THE EFFECTS
OF THE INTERNET
ON SOCIAL
RELATIONSHIPS

THE EFFECTS OF THE INTERNET ON SOCIAL RELATIONSHIPS

THERAPEUTIC CONSIDERATIONS

Joan D. Atwood, Ph.D., LMFT, LCSW* &

Conchetta Gallo, Ph.D., LMFT#

iUniverse, Inc.
Bloomington

* Joan D. Atwood, Ph.D., LMFT, LCSW is a Professor of Marriage and Family Therapy and is the CEO and Clinical Director of Marriage and Family Therapists of New York. She can be reached at jatwood@optonline.net http://www.NYMFT.Com

Conchetta Gallo, Ph.D., LMFT works for the New York State Board of Education. She is also a Marriage and Family Therapist for NYMFT.

The Effects of the Internet on Social Relationships
Therapeutic Considerations

iUniverse books may be ordered through booksellers or by contacting:

iUniverse
1663 Liberty Drive
Bloomington, IN 47403
www.iuniverse.com
1-800-Authors (1-800-288-4677)

ISBN: 978-1-4620-4704-8 (sc)
ISBN: 978-1-4620-4705-5 (ebk)

Printed in the United States of America

iUniverse rev. date: 10/24/2011

CONTENTS

THE EFFECTS OF THE INTERNET ON SOCIAL RELATIONSHIPS

Nothing is permanent but change (Heraclitus, 4th century)

Technology has brought forth a paradigm shift in how we conceptualize, define and engage in social relationships. The internet, along with the abundance of constantly evolving immersive media and wireless technologies, has not only revolutionized how we communicate and connect in our world but also when, where and with whom. It has been said that the degrees between virtual life and one's "true" experienced reality increasingly overlap, with every new advancement. Technology has revolutionized communication and brought the world together and it has done so with the ease of a single click.

Historically, the Internet became available to users around 1993—not even 30 years ago. Prior to that, it was used primarily by computer scientists, engineers, librarians and military personnel. It was brought into the universities around 1970;an early form of email was adopted in the early 70s. Around that time, the TCP/IP architecture was developed and the structure and usage of the internet was simplified. UNIX was developed at Bell Labs in 1978 allowing for user and discussion groups. Now, information was exchanged throughout the world and non-technical people became users of email and the Internet. In 1994, the World Wide Web was designed to develop standards for the Internet; AOL, Prodigy, and CompuServe appeared. In June of 2010, there were 266,224,500 users, representing 78% of the population. The United States has the highest number of Internet users in the world. It has revolutionized the way people communicate and relate with each other.

Increasingly, clients come for therapy because of Internet behavior. Adolescents are brought in by parents because they stay up too late on the Internet. Parents bring their teens in because of texting behavior or because they looked at their children's My Space or Facebook and did not like what they saw. Young women come to therapy because they are tired of meeting "losers" online and are unsatisfied with their dating lives. Couples come for therapy for a host of reasons such as emotional connections made on the Internet that are threatening to the couple relationship, internet infidelity, affairs that happen as a result of finding someone on the Internet, or pornography use or overuse. These are the issues increasingly brought to therapists' offices.

The purpose of this book is to explore the effects of the Internet on relationships. The relationships examined are adolescents, dating relationships, and couple and marital relationships. In addition, since pornography is also a click away, the effects of pornography are explored as well. The implications for therapy are considered throughout.

Chapter one, The Connecting Internet explores the whole notion of Connection. Communication patterns and even language has changed as a result of the Internet. The way we socially connect has changed drastically; even language has changed as a result of the Internet. The chapter presents the differences between the genders in terms of Internet usage, as well as the changing norms. It looks at social addiction and gives an overview of online dating and internet infidelity.

Chapter two, Adolescents, the Internet, and Sexuality, begins by stating, "For today's youth, access to the Internet is a right, not a privilege." Adolescents have access to the Internet through laptops, cell phones, iPods and iPads. These mobile devices allow for a 24/7 connection to the Internet. How does this constant access influence adolescents? How does it affect their psychological development and their socialization? How does the increased exposure to the peer group affect their behavior? Their psycho-social development? Adolescent romantic relationships? Does adolescent cybersex become relevant? This chapter presents the statistics of Adolescent usage and the types of behaviors adolescents engage in vis-à-vis the Internet. It provides information for parents, ending with a discussion of therapeutic and life cycle stage implications. Treatment considerations are then considered.

Chapter three, The Effects of Internet Related Pornographic Viewing on Adolescents and the Implications for Mental Health Professionals, looks at the effects of pornographic viewing by adolescents. The chapter presents information on adolescent internet usage and the varying perspectives on this usage. It explores gender differences, focusing on the variations in males and females. There is a section on the effects of viewing pornography on adolescents. Assessment techniques for mental health professionals are then presented, along with treatment options.

Chapter four, The Effects of Online Dating and Mating in Romantic Relationships, explores the socio-demographics of online dating and the typical ways singles meet other singles on the Internet. The Chapter first provides a history of internet dating, exploring the characteristics of online daters, as well as the positive and negative aspects of Internet dating. There is a section on the Ten Commandments for Online Daters. The Chapter also explores the difference between offline and online dating.

Chapter five, The Internet and Romantic Relationships: Help or Hindrance? explores the ways the Internet can help and or hinder primary relationships. It explores the norms and social mores for primary relationships regarding the Internet and examines the concept of monogamy. Gender differences are presented as well as the risk factors. Treatment options and implications are considered.

Chapter six, Cyber-Affairs: What's the Big Deal? Therapeutic Considerations, states that it can be estimated that 50-60% of married men and 45-55% of married women engage in extramarital sex at some time or another during their marriage and almost half come to therapy because of it. Online infidelity accounts for a growing trend in reasons given for divorce according to the President of the American Academy of Matrimonial Lawyers, and it is believed that it has been greatly underestimated. Because of the unfamiliarity and newness of this type of infidelity, mental health professionals are often unfamiliar with the dynamics associated with the concept of cyber-affairs and "virtual cheating." Many in fact do not consider the behavior as infidelity. This chapter explores this phenomenon, the cyber-affair, and examines the factors influencing it, the unique problems associated with this type of affair, along with a discussion of the therapeutic considerations.

Chapter seven, Pornography and Its Effects on Relationships, looks at the 21st century and the accessibility of pornography on the Internet. Statistics are presented (17.5 million surfers visited porn sites from their homes in January, 2000). This Chapter presents also the facts and figures of Pornographic use. The positive and negative aspects of pornography are explored. Religious and cultural implications are examined. Treatment Considerations are presented.

Chapter eight, Couples Dealing with Heavy Pornographic Use, offers a case history of a couple struggling with heavy pornographic use.

Joan D. Atwood, Ph.D., LMFT, LCSW & Conchetta Gallo, Ph.D., LMFT

The Chapter points out that there is a lack of research on this particular type of compulsion even though it is a common problem and one that mental health professionals face often. Treatment options and goals are presented.

CHAPTER 1

The Internet: An Overview

Scott Fishkind
Irene Gallego,
Jennifer Goldenberg

Across the lifespan, associative and attachment bonds have clear survival and reproductive advantages that help explain the motivation to form and maintain close social bonds. Just as hunger and thirst motivate the search for food and water, the pain of unmet social needs and social isolation motivates a search for social connection. The desire for connection is so irrepressible that people imagine relationships with important social others, or indulge in "social snacks" (e.g., photos of loved ones) and surrogates (e.g., parasocial attachments to television characters) (Cacioppo, 2009).

The means by which we obtain and maintain social connections is reflective of our culture and has implications for societal function. With the advent of the Internet, the means by which we obtain and maintain social connections has become infinitely greater. The Internet provides numerous avenues to network and connect socially, tailoring preferences to unique specificities. Looking for a friend? Click. Looking for a date? Click. Looking for advice? Click. Looking to sell or buy something? Click. Click. Click.

One click of the computer mouse and you have invariable connected with infinite people in infinite corners of the earth. In fact, the social capability of the Internet has redefined what it means to connect.

Sociability has become so entrenched in the Internet that internet language is finding its way into the common vernacular. Internet language is comprised of distinctive written features, primarily acronyms, abbreviations, and respellings. Internet language emerges from standard language ideology and deterministic views of technology, where the definition of these features as both nonstandard and internet-specific articulates the perceived distinctiveness of internet interactions (Squires, 2010).

With our means of communication ever transforming and augmenting, relationships will invariably transform as well. Social networking websites such as Facebook and MySpace help people reconnect and stay connected with individuals they may not have otherwise communicated with. Further, the abundant array of online dating websites now allows individuals to connect romantically where they would otherwise not have an opportunity to do so. The constant connection and myriad choices of connections can complicate relationships in unforeseen ways. Some people may have trouble navigating this new frontier of social life; boundaries of propriety must be re-drawn and social meanings must be rethought and redefined. Couples interacting online may have to readjust their thoughts on and feelings about what constitutes fidelity and when words or images online cross an emotional threshold. The desire to connect online may or may not be reflective of an individual's desire to emotionally connect with another individual, or commit "cyber infidelity". Fear of the unknown, fear of an online world that has temptation lurking, may increasingly become the cause for relational strife.

The Internet has permanently changed the dating landscape. In the U.S. alone, tens of millions of people are trying to find dates or spouses online every day (Epstein, 2009). This is not a passing phenomenon either; the future of online dating looks very bright. Interest is growing quickly, and intense competition will force rapid changes in the kinds of services that are offered. In 2001 online dating was a $40-million business; by 2008 that figure was expected to reach $600 million, with more than 800 businesses vying for every dollar (Epstein 2009).

The Online Population

The role of gender roles has always had a significant impact on the way couples relate to each other. Defined gender roles may serve to help or hinder a couple's ability to communicate and emote. Gender roles are a significant variable in the study of Internet use as well. Helsper (2010) points out that gender differences may exist in the skills used for the Internet, as well as the actual use of the Internet. For instance, research has found that females primarily focus on communicative Internet use while males primarily focus on entertaining Internet use (Helsper, 2010). While use of the internet for communication and entertainment may overlap, males appear to focus on Internet games and sexual content, while women appear to focus on health information (Helsper, 2010). This implies that there are differences in the role that Internet plays in the lives of women and men. This further implies that men and women may be using similar networks for varying purposes.

Helsper (2010) found that men integrate technologies more broadly into their everyday lives than women. This implies that men would be more likely to engage in online activity due to their natural inclination towards technology. Not surprisingly then, Hargittai (2007) points out that it has been found that men have more skills than women in Internet use. Further, online shopping appears to be primarily a male activity in spite of the fact that offline shopping appears to be a primarily female activity (Helsper, 2010). Internet use for sexual material was primarily a male area of focus; however, marital status did influence male use where divorced men were "especially likely to look for sexual material" (Helsper, 2010, p. 368).

Such findings signify that social networks are used by women more to maintain connections and to communicate while they are used by men to discover prospective connections, whether for business or pleasure. Hargittai (2007) found that more women than men in the college age used social networking sites, implying that the primary use of these sites is to communicate. In spite of the differences in men and women's use of the Internet for social networking, research also identified that there was not a significant difference in their use of blogging web sites. However, it was found that older college students use social networking sites less frequently than younger college students (Hargittai, 2007). Such findings signify that the older populations, such as 20-29 year olds, may be focusing on other priorities such as entering the work force.

The Internet, and internet privacy issues, has become integral for both employers and job-seekers. Employers now use the Internet to gather information about prospective employees; employers can track the social behaviors of Internet users like never before. While access to information has proven useful for employers, it can be detrimental to those employees whose online behavior can signifies warning signs

Computers: A Foreign Language

In cyberspace individuals are confronted with numerous types of computer-related terminology and phrases, To some, especially new Internet users, this may seem like a foreign language. Computer Mediated Communication (CMC) is a term that defines the way people communicate through the Internet. People can communicate through emails or social networks or numerous modes of cyber-interaction. Internet Relay Chat (IRC) is a term that describes a type of social interaction that occurs through the Internet but is conducted almost in real time. That is the key difference between CMC and IRC (Paolillo, 1999). IRC can have multiple participants at the same time, and the message length is generally short, much like a conversation people would have in face-to-face communication. IRC systems were the gateway into our now modern day instant messaging sites such as AIM and Skype (Paolillo, 1999).

Internet terminology has developed to refer specifically to online social activity; "Internet browsing" is one such term. Internet browsing is different from social browsing in that social appears to be synonymous with the term social searching.

Changing and Maintaining Norms.

Alongside changes in linguistic terminology, computer-related language is becoming more normative. Thus, conversational enactments are created online in different ways, indicated by either an asterisk or an arrow sign such as the enactment North (2007) uses: "Mockturtle: <tries to think of a witty response> <fails>"; this is an example of an individual, expressing that he or she was trying to think of a response because the person could not see him or her acting thoughtfully.

Conversations online now mimic face-to-face conversations, even though individuals cannot see or hear body language and facial reactions. Such facilities have evolved from simply imitating real life conversation to expressing feelings in the form of online "statuses" on Facebook and the like, and "away messages" on instant messaging mediums that keep individual's social network constantly in touch with a their feelings, thoughts and daily activities.

Online communication allows of mimicking of types of environments, such as Carnival environments (North, 2007). These types of atmospheres allow for identities to be "masked, their social hierarchy is suspended, and speech norms are relaxed", which can lead to playfulness and creativity in what one says to someone in the midst of a conversation. According to North (2007), there has been an increase of the "ambivalent use of profanity and abusive language" used online.). Through this creativity, individuals have been combining existing elements in their language and creating novel acronyms as well as other words, which have become characteristic of online language and Internet communication. This fosters the development of a main group identity, especially for chat room groups, and that the social context is co-constructed by those who are part of the group (North, 2007).

Thus, other norms of communication have been affected through forms of online communication, such as chat rooms or social sites.

Norms of creativity and playfulness in a conversation have found room for enhancement. In fact, norms are even created in the group or chat room being used, and those in the group construct the social context itself. An identity of the group is formed this way, and allows for linguistic creativity (North, 2007). Many facial expressions were created this way, such as typed smiley faces or "emoticons", and acronyms, such as "LOL" meaning to "laugh out loud" were created all to mean different things. Emoticons are facial expressions pictorially represented by punctuation and letters, usually to express a writer's mood. Emoticons are often used to alert a responder to the tenor or temper of a statement, and can change and improve interpretation of plain text. The word is a portmanteau of the English words *emotion* (or *emote*) and *icon* (Emoticon, 2011).

Many of these forms of communication have become universal in the online world. It then becomes evident that social comfort and convenience are key elements of the online social networking experience.

Socialization Comfort and Convenience

Online social networking provides a comfortable base to build upon existing offline connections and to create new connections the world over. Additionally, computer-related language makes communicating much more punctuated and convenience. Thus, the popularity of social networking websites has grown greatly in the recent years (Hargittai, 2007). Online networking originally began with e-mailing and instant messaging in chat-rooms on sites such as with AOL, Yahoo, and MSN Messenger. Social networking then grew to include video chatting through web-cams and servers like Skype. Now, these sites that have created visible online circles that other individuals can easily see with a click of their mouse. Websites like Chatroulette pairs random strangers from around the world together for webcam-based conversations. Visitors to the website randomly begin an online chat (video, audio and text) with another visitor. At any point, either user may leave the current chat by initiating another random connection (Chatroulette, 2011).

These sites include not only the social networking sites (e.g. Facebook, Friendster, MySpace, Twitter, etc.), but also dating sites like Match.com, and numerous blogs like Xanga. Some websites, like Facebook, originated for certain communities such as colleges (Walther et al, 2008). The expansion of these types of websites provides a broad base of members from which a person can shop to add to their own group of online friends. Further, these websites provide ways in which a person can connect with people they already know, and reconnect with people they used to know. Searches through e-mails, names, personalized html links, and friends associations provides incredible links to almost all members of these sites.

In addition to sweeping access online, people now carry PDAs (Personal Digital Assistants), mobile devices that often have the ability to connect to the Internet. PDAs like the Blackberry and iPhone have their own messaging system to connect its own users through PIN numbers. This messaging system also uses the status feature, allowing people to keep track of each other's thoughts, feelings, and physical whereabouts.

Moreover, the majority of PDAs have applications for online social networking websites like Facebook and MySpace so that the user can access compacted versions of the sites adapted to the mobile user. With such constant and instantaneous access to connections in the online world, there are clearly implications of Internet use that vary across the spectrum of positivity and negativity. They range from probing the "potential gains and harms" to the role "identity construction and expression to the building and maintenance of social capital" (Hargittai, 2007, p. 276).

The ways in which we connect and communicate with others will invariably affect the way people speak and write to one another. Research shows that there is a change in the way people type/write to one another through the IRC systems. For instance, many people turn to shorthand by substituting single letters for entire words, such as "r" for "are" and "u" for "you," as well as customizing the spelling of words such as by typing a "z" instead of an "s" (Paolillo, 1999).

Another type of shorthand often used in chat rooms or IRC's are acronyms, such as "wb" which means welcome back, "LOL" which means laughing out loud, and "ROFL" which means "rolling on the floor laughing". These shorthand messages came about as an adoption to allow the Internet users to economize keystrokes (Paolillo, 2001). This has become a norm in communicating through these channels, regardless of the fact that these people have never met face to face, and the people on these channels can be constantly changing (Paolillo, 1999). This type of communication is becoming normative in large part because the majority of social networking now occurs online; it affects how people socialize and how frequently they socialize.

Thus, the way in which we use language to achieve connection morphs even faster due to the frequency people are online and how often these sites are used. At the end of the day, people are and will always be social beings where their motivations for joining social networks stays the same (Coyle & Vaughn, 2008).

Constant Connection and Information Access

Humans are innately interested in the human nature of their peers. With the advent of online social media, it appears as though people are becoming increasingly interested in the lives, feelings, thoughts and whereabouts of their peers, their family and friends, and their general social connections. With heightened access to this information, we inevitably know and learn more about our social network than previously known. This level of transparency online has given allowed users to find new and more abundant ways to keep tabs on their friends, and more importantly, their partners.

The ease with which we now connect and the instantaneous availability of information will invariable be a cause for concern for some. According to a poll given by womansavers.com, over seventy percent of all women feel that emotional affairs could lead to physical affairs (Alexander, 2009). Thus, it is also not surprising that these same seventy percent of woman feel that internet "chatting" can become emotional and can lead to real life encounters with potential mates/lovers, and potentially result in infidelity (Alexander, 2009). In addition to infidelity, there are numerous concerns about the development of addictions derived from Internet use, as well as concerns about what previously existing addictions potentially transform into in the online social world. According to Rimskii (2010), internet users can develop the kind of Internet addiction in which communication for the sake of interaction comes to be seen as the supreme value; individuals experience anxiety if they do not log on after a relatively brief time, do not check for messages in blogs and email, do not watch the news, and so on.

Social Addiction

With 1.5 billion Internet users around the world today, the Internet has become an integral part of our society. With the now ubiquitous use of the Internet, researchers have become interested new disorders relating to computer addiction or Internet addiction disorders (Jaffe, 2010). According to Jaffe (2010), Internet addiction disorder (IAD) is a controversial term being used to describe problematic use of the Internet. Many wonder if excessive Internet use really counts as an addiction as IAD is not yet a recognized diagnosis in the Diagnostic and Statistical Manual of Mental Disorders IV-TR (DSM IV). According to Jaffe (2010), people are most likely to develop unhealthy Internet habits using online social applications such as e-mail, instant messaging, and networking sites (e.g. Facebook, MySpace). Chat rooms and massively multiplayer online role playing games (MMORPGs) are especially addicting as they allow a user to instantly communicate with hundreds if not thousands of other users (Parsons, 2005). Aside from this, other forms of addiction bring concerns.

From the addiction of internet pornography to the addictions of mere internet use, the Internet is clearly has addictive properties. The internet allows individuals to create and maintain their social worlds in ways unforeseen the world over. Like any addiction, the cost for people addicted to the internet in any form is evident in the quality of their social function and relationships with others.

Enhancing and Expanding Social Circles

Whether connections are made for business, friendship or love, it is evident that the instantaneous nature of the internet serves a purpose to those who seek it. With the rise of online social networking, there is also a substantial increase in the uncertainty of social processes and phenomena; they exhibit randomness, great variability, and alternativeness (Rimskii, 2010). Social support systems multiply as instantaneous connections with family and friends from around the world are now possible. The prospects for dating, friendship, and business networking become exponential, In terms of its content and functionality, the Internet is a rich means of information activity and communication of the kind that always go on in particular social groups (Rimskii,2010). On the Internet, individuals are united by their shared activity, engaged in working with information and communicating on interests and priorities that they care about. Members of these new social groups do not usually get together in the real world;

what they share is their active involvement on the Internet (Rimskii, 2010).

Research indicates that computer-mediated social networks affects a person's offline social networks. Internet users may have larger social networks and that the Internet itself has helped to sustain a person's social networks (Coyle & Vaughn, 2008). For instance, Coyle & Vaughn (2008) found that college students were using one social network (i.e. Facebook) to help keep in contact with people such as past classmates. Moreover, college students use Facebook to engage in social searching, to find individuals they may have just met or, and meet new people as well whom they would like to meet. This is just one example of how a social networking site can help to expand a person's social capital and expand their social networks as well as help maintain it by keeping someone in touch with their acquaintances and friends from high school (Coyle & Vaughn, 2008).

Online Romance

Wildermuth and Vogl-Bauer (2007) found that the average Internet consumer spends seventy percent of his or her time building their personal relationships. These include online friends, sexual partnerships, and romances. According to Parks and Roberts (1998), over ninety-three percent of Internet users participate in some sort of online relationship and about twenty-six percent of those relationships are romantic ones. That means about a quarter of people who use the Internet, find romantic partners through cyberspace. Thus, according to Parks and Roberts (1998), one in every four Internet users has the Internet to thank for their romantic partners.

Romantic online relationships can be just as strong and emotionally bonding as relationships that are offline regardless of the physical limitation of the technology. Wildermuth and Vogl-Bauer (2007) show how online relationships can still evoke powerful emotions, both positive and negative, even though there was no physical factor involved in the relationship. Many individuals in that study described their "love, happiness, fear, anger, and sadness resulting from their online romances" (Wildermuth & Vogl-Bauer, 2007, p.221).

With the advent of internet romance, the potential for intimacy becomes more likely for those people who are less sociable in the "offline" world.

The Internet allows for people who have a more introverted personality to communicate online and branch out in their social spheres in a way that allows introverts to feel more comfortable when communicating (Sheeks & Birchmeier, 2007). This might allow introverted individual more opportunities to attain romantic relationships where their personalities would otherwise prevent. Thus, the Internet has allowed for users to expand their social networks exponentially.

The Online Daters

Online dating seems to be more prevalent in the younger population than in the older population; individuals between eighteen and twenty-nine years old are the most common users (Stephure, Boon, MacKinnon, & Deveau, 2009). Nonetheless, older populations can and do find the appeal of online dating. As Stephure et al. (2009) point out, "the sheer volume of the user base, the speed, and the convenience of use associated with online personals ads are more appealing to older people than to younger people". (). This may be due to the fact that older people have already established their social world in the offline community. However, older people are more likely to be divorced or separated and re-entering the dating world (Stephure, et al., 2009, p. 661). Thus, it appears that older individuals could benefit more from the online dating world to expand their social base. However, as Stephure et al. (2009) note, the use of technology for this purpose may seem unconventional to many older adults and they may be less skilled than their younger counterparts at Internet use.

However, this may be changing as the older generations become more educated about the use of the Internet for social purposes. In fact, Stephure et al. (2009) found that older individuals did, in fact, engage in online dating more so than younger individuals. Furthermore, these older individuals were more likely to seriously seek "marital and sexual partners online" (Stephure, et al., 2009, p. 673). Thus, a younger population may be using online dating to establish romantic relationships in a less serious manner, perhaps for casual dating or sexual encounters

Research also found that individuals pursuing online dating were not as happy with their offline opportunities (Stephure, et al., 2009). This seemed to be related to age, where older people were less satisfied in offline chances to meet people, except in printed personal ads (Stephure, et al., 2009). In addition, it appears that the stigma with online dating may be diminishing. Seventy percent of these individuals tell their friends and family they are using online dating services (Stephure, et al., 2009). This implies the online world of romance is becoming more normative and less associated with shame and desperation.

As Wildermuth and Vogl-Bauer (2007) suggest, the Internet influences the messages available to consumers due purely textual data influencing users' initial decision about possible relational developments. This makes the content of the messages received more essential than if there were physical cues the person could take into account. Wildermuth and Vogl-Bauer (2007) also found that it was common for Internet users to increase the amount of information available to them about their partner through other mediums, such as calling them on the phone to hear their voice, or eventually even meeting them face-to-face. Once the online relationship strengthens, the individuals would want to expand upon and enhance their relational experience through these other modalities of interactions.

Moreover, social networking is not just a way of developing a new relationships, it is another way for people to interact with existing romantic partners. A pre-existing relationship could evolve and eventually add online exchanges to the relationship as one more way of connecting and interacting. Thus, aside from transforming or revolutionizing communication and how people interact, the Internet also allows for the expansion upon that which what already exists. Unfortunately, the Internet magnifies negative aspects of offline relationships as well. Communication on the Internet can deprive users of the nonverbal component of communication, with consequences that are far from unequivocal. In particular, communication on the Internet can distort the meaning of messages; there is more opportunity to manipulate the consciousness of those who receive information sent by some user (Rimskii, 2010).

Romantic Ambiguity

The Internet not only allows new romantic relationships to develop, it sets the ground for previous lovers to reconnect. Individuals often maintain contact with partners from their past in the form of online friendships, as well as have friends their current partner does not know (Muise, Christofides, & Desmaraise, 2009). As Muise et al. (2009) note, this contact creates many "ambiguous scenes" that commonly trigger jealousy in the newer relationship. In fact, participants in their study describe feeling an "addiction" to continuously screening the websites of their past partners and current partners (Muise et al, 2009, p. 443). This addiction could lead prolonged jealousy and relationship problems. Although Muise et al's study was conducted with college students, such findings are important for the general population as more and more individuals are creating accounts in the social networking world. With infinite links to their past partners and relationships, married couples can surely be faced with similar jealousy issues that prove to be more serious, perhaps escalating to the couple's divorce.

Aside from online interactions, relationships are already affected by jealousy. The meanings that social cues have, for a greeting or a hug, can be confounded depending on the person interpreting them. Social networking websites delineate social clues more readily; they "provide easy access to . . . partner's information, including changes to their profiles, additions of new contacts . . . , and messages posted on their page" (Muise, et al., 2009, p. 441). Such information only fosters, if not enhances, feelings a jealousy. Muise et al., (2009) note that levels of self-esteem and levels of trust in one's partner influence jealousy issues. Thus, lower levels of individual self-esteem and lower levels of trust increase jealousy (Muise, et al., 2009). Time spent monitoring these social cues may be related to increased levels jealousy. These factors are important because online social networks allow people to obtain more information about their significant others than they would have been able to access without the online networks (Muise, et al., 2009). However, as in the "real" world, the cues and means are often ambiguous.

Online Infidelity

Online infidelity is becoming a bigger issue as access and social ambiguities increase opportunity for cheating (Kalish, 2009). Online infidelity may be known as: cyber affairs, cyber cheating, online affairs, Internet affairs, and Internet infidelity, amongst many others. All of these terms apply to the same thing: a romantic affair involving intimate or sexually explicit communication between two people, one of whom is married or in a committed relationship, which is conducted primarily in cyberspace or over the internet (Houston, 2006). In her book, *The Truth About Cyber Affairs and Online Infidelity,* Ruth Houston writes that "The

Internet has removed the risk. Now it can all be done in cyberspace. A few clicks of the mouse will vie a potential cheater instant access to an endless array of willing partners, in his or her local area, or around the world".

According to a poll of over 1,000 woman conducted by womansavers. com, approximately fifty-one percent of women believed that viewing porn was emotional cheating (Alexander, 2009). In another of their polls, sixty-three percent of all woman reported that they felt online affairs constituted infidelity (Alexander, 2009). Although it may be clear that there has been a distinguishable difference between emotional and physical affairs, the bottom line is that the Internet has become an endless outlet for emotional and/or non-physical affairs to blossom. These "affairs" have been a product of many different social media outlets that have evolved in the last several years such as the previously mentioned Facebook, MySpace, Friendster, and Twitter. Further, emotional affairs surely have the potential to become physical affairs.

New research by a UK-based extramarital dating website, IllicitEncounters.com, has reinforced claims that Facebook is fast becoming the method to conduct affairs. An IllicitEncounters.com survey reported that over sixty-one percent of the people surveyed said a text or Internet post had at some point either incriminated them totally or aroused suspicion about their affair to their other half (Hartley, 2008). The use of channels such as Facebook have also created a "social normality or way of acting" when using the website (Hartley, 2008). For instance, people who are on social media websites like Facebook have un-written code of ethics and morals that stand by their use of the site. For these users, a person is not officially in a committed relationship until the individual's relationship status is changed on Facebook to let everyone know, hence the popularized phrase "It's not official if it's not on Facebook."

Until displayed on Facebook, the two individuals are unofficially just "hanging out" or "hooking up." When a person visits his or her home screen on Facebook, friends' relationship status updates show up on the news feed. For example, the update would read "Billy is now in a relationship" or "Billy has changed his relationship status to *Complicated*." Conversations that once took place between a couple about the relationship status, such as the seriousness of the relationship and the level of commitment established, are now administered by pulling a drop down menu and asking for a virtual relationship confirmation. For the people who still have their ex-girlfriends or ex-boyfriends as "friends" on Facebook, they can see when their ex is dating a new person or when that person ex breaks up with their current significant other. This level of involvement may be overwhelming and completely novel for many people. It has become increasingly difficult to separate yourself from past partners and lovers, and as a result, an individual's present relationship may be affected. Denoting the prevalence of such infidelitous relationships, Kalish (2009) writes:

> "According to my research participants in several phases of my study, there are more extramarital affairs in this population now than in the 1990's, before the Web, search engines, classmates sites, and now social networking were invented. In the 1990's, people who looked up lost loves did so very purposefully. People were easy to find—it is a myth that only the Internet has brought long lost loves back together—but to contact that old flame, it was necessary to make human contact: perhaps asking a friend or relative of the lost love for his/her phone number and then calling the lost love at home. It was a rare married man who had the audacity to go to an elder parent to ask for the daughter's phone number, and then call his lost love at home, not knowing if an irritated spouse would answer the phone. And the act of making that inquiry or phone call was clearly a romantic overture, and the searcher knew it. No rationalizations there".

The Internet is now casual, even accidental; Facebook may "suggest" you befriend someone you have mutual friends with, or a picture of an ex may appear on your homepage because you have mutual Facebook friends. There is very little you can do avoid cyber interactions with people in your online social circle. Further, individuals new to online networking may not understand the transparency and exposure they are giving former partners, or the Pandora's Box they are opening by befriending someone online.

Before Facebook and other social networking sites, a lost love could be found through Google, web sites like Classmates.com, or people finder sites like Zabasearch.com, etc. Social networking sites do not cause divorce or infidelity, but they can certainly enable it As Kalish (2009) points out, "infidelity already exists. It appears that Facebook and other online social networks simply set up the stage for infidelity opportunities to expand greatly".

Distance and Deceit

While online social networking creates numerous y outlets for connection and communication, it also has the ability to create distance. Social relationships, by their very nature, are transactional. They are richly imbued with nuance, color and tone. Relationships engaged in the various theaters of social media, even when those relationships exist in a coincident social milieu, lack these characteristics. This is due in part because social media introduces two parallel and paradoxical elements: false intimacy and social distance. These elements contribute to the fostering of relationships that in their lack of authenticity can sometimes be at best awkward and that, at other times, in their consequences be at worst tragic.

There is a science fiction novel by Orson Scott Card (1985) called *Ender's Game* in which children are taught to be fighter pilots in an intergalactic war by playing a video game that simulates combat. The tragedy of the story is that Ender, the hero and victim of the tale, eventually puzzles out that it's not a game at all, and that he and his playmates are actually controlling drones pitted against an unseen and unknown enemy in full-scale battle. This is a perfect metaphor for social distance as fostered by people's experience of social media: it is on a screen, so it can't be real or, more properly, it doesn't carry the same weight or social valence as it would were it occurring in vivo.

Social media also offers a sense of false intimacy. Somehow it has become important for a person to know that his or her "friend," whom he or she may not have actually seen in thirty years, just went for a walk and somehow it is important that this friend tell this individual, and 250 other "friends." But now this person knows about her day, and that somehow fosters a sense of connection for everyone. It is this same false sense of connection that can prompt even people with the most rigid of boundaries to become flexible within contexts of dating sites like E-Harmony, Match.com, etc. The real misfortune here is not that social distance has people saying or doing inappropriate things, or that false intimacy has people falling in love with a fantasy. Rather, the real misfortune is that these elements and the entire fabric of what makes up media-informed social interactions are working whether independently or together to contribute to a fairly significant deficit and declination in social and emotional intelligence all around. Thus, it is crucial to take note of what aspects of deceit present in the online world are contributing to the social intelligence.

The Online Alter Ego

We all search for ideal partners, the Internet now allows you to expand your network of "ideals" to the many users available to you on Internet dating sites. According to Wu and Chiou (2009), more options lead Internet users to "accelerate processing by reducing time spent on each alternative profile". This also leads to reducing the Internet users' cognitive resources that in turns leads to not being able to ignore irrelevant information. The overload of cognitions also leads to poor choices in sacrificing some traits the person originally desired in finding in their potential partner.

In searching, it is important to realize that other people contribute photographs and comments on an individual's profile, therefore the social connections revealed by online networks may also impact a person's perceived attractiveness (Walther, et al., 2008). Walther et al. (2008) point out the context effect of the Internet. The context effect implies that an individual's physical attractiveness can either increase or decrease depending on the people associated with him or her. Walther et al. (2008) call this the "assimilation effect". When presented with no link to each other, a person was rated average in attractiveness when compared to others who were more or less attractive (Walther, et al., 2008). As a result, one would assume this person would be rated average at all times.

However, according to Walther et al. (2008), that same person was rated as more attractive when linked to others who were more attractive. On the other hand, when linked to others who were less attractive, that person was rated as less attractive (Walther, et al., 2008). Thus, the perspective of a person's attractiveness seemingly varies depending on their social circle. Thus, this concept provides important considerations for people using the Internet as a dating tool.

Further, there has been a relationship between physical attractiveness and positive personality impressions (Walther, et al., 2008, p. 36). Despite belief factual basis to this belief, the general idea is that beautiful people are also good people (Walther, et al., 2008). Consequently, the publicized aspect of an individual's Internet social circles can perhaps even hinder their prospective dating opportunities. Such factors are important because "online dating is a widespread and popular activity" that "generate[s] nearly US $470 million" (Stephure, et al., 2009, p. 659). With these numbers and 40 million new users a month, online dating ranks number one in revenue of paid online content (Stephure, et al., 2009).

Alongside exaggerated interpretations of personal appearance, individuals using online dating sites may be wary of the level of truth inherent in users' personal disclosures. For instance, individuals may have the ability to doctor their appears by enlisting software such as Photoshop to manipulate the way they are portrayed. As Wildermuth and Vogl-Bauer (2007) pointed out, the limitation of the Internet for allowing users to being able to verify stories they are told about the individuals they are interacting with and creating romantic relationships with could possibly encourage the users to "engage in strategic self-enhancement". Consequently, consumers may present themselves in a more positive light and enhance their attributes. This idea of less fear of repercussions through not being able to verify their stories helps explain the large rate of online affairs that Wildermuth and Vogl-Bauer (2007) found in their study.

The ambiguous nature associated with online dating networking may deter some users from embarking in such endeavors. However, as Wildermuth and Vogl-Bauer (2007) showed in their study, people seek "significant consistency across partner messages so that they can feel secure in the assessment of their partner". For example, if a person is fearful of progressing to the next stage of intimacy with his or her online romantic partner, they could cross-reference past e-mails or online communications and connections to look for incongruities. Contrarily, and on a more positive note, people can also share enriching information about themselves on these sites, through videos or pictures, in addition to instant messaging or talking over the phone (Coyle & Vaughn, 2008).

According to Wu and Chiou (2009), the more options a person has, the more searching the person do, which in turns decreases their choice quality almost as if the person becomes overwhelmed and their cognitive abilities to choose a potential partner of good quality for them is lowered. With the overload of options, irrelevant information increases the likelihood of the person becoming distracted or attracted to attributes on the profiles, which were not relevant to their original preferences. Furthermore, this overload of options leaves some feeling overwhelmed over the inability to control even what they themselves present to the online social world through their own profiles.

Privacy Concerns

Aside from the benefits of instantaneous connections, there are important implications for privacy. Individuals may become confounded or lost in the appeal of the Internet's bottomless fulfillment for the human connection and interaction. Regardless, the Internet has clearly revolutionized the social world, and it is crucial that we explore these societal changes.

Making a first impression is contingent on both the information you provide and the way in which that information is interpreted. Social networking sites complicate first impressions because it is the other people who "contribute information" to a person's profile and wall that impacts others' first impressions of the person as well (Walther, et al., 2008). Thus, "the possibility that individuals may be judged on the basis of others' behaviors in such spaces prompts this question: Are we known by the company we keep?" (Walther, et al., 2008, p. 29). Such publicized activity can hold serious implications for people in monogamous, committed relationships. Thus, the potential for relationship problems only expands through the impact of others' behaviors.

Further pointing out the issue of privacy concerns, Govani and Pashley (2005) point out that people may feel safe from behind the screens of their computers but have, in actuality, no privacy. Many of these websites ask information that is personal. Facebook, in particular, provides information that puts people at risk of being the victim of identity theft or being stalked (Govani & Pashley, 2005). In fact, as Govani and Pashley (2005) point out, it uses a person's full name, with about a rate of eighty-nine percent validity of name provided. Furthermore, it allows members to provide information such as addresses and phone numbers that are used in identity theft (Govani & Pashley, 2005). While not every member provides every piece of information, many may overly trust the security of such websites to guard their information. Thus, many do accurately provide this information (Govani & Pashley, 2005). Some people face short-term consequences for the material displayed on such website. For instance, sexual and drug posts have led to family disappointment and even police intervention (Govani & Pashley, 2005). In addition, many people who use websites like Facebook do not think about the long-term consequences of its use, as it may be related to future employment, potential for child adoption, etc.

Uncensored and possibly explicit photos that are uploaded and linked to people on such websites and uncensored conversation posted on walls can become issues. Interestingly, Walther et al. (2008) found that the "sexual double standard" still holds true in the online world. This means that men whose profiles have postings and linked pictures that display premarital sexuality received more positive social judgments than those of women's with the same type of sexual content (Walther, et al., 2008). This further highlights the implications of the highly publicized social world and the importance of privacy concerns

Further, people forget that information, including pictures and videos posted on Facebook, is easily identifiable through public searches on Google and search engines of the like. Govani and Pashley (2005) note that such information can be used by potential employers as well as by the government as a judgment of the individual's character. According to Govani and Pashley (2005) about eighty-four percent of online social networking users are aware of privacy settings that can be adjusted. In spite of this awareness, about half of these people actually enable the privacy settings (Govani & Pashley, 2005).

Aside from becoming educated about internet privacy, some people attempt to control the expansion of their online social network. In what claims to be the first study of its kind, Christopher Sibona, a doctoral student in the Computer Science and Information Systems program at the University of Denver, looked at the reasons why people get "de-friended", wherein a friend removes their virtual connection to you, on Facebook (Rael, 2010). His study, which was conducted on the online social network Twitter, consisted of a survey of more than 1,500 Facebook users. Sibona found that the top three reasons for de-friending people were: frequent unimportant posts, polarizing posts (e.g. bringing up religion or politics), and inappropriate posts (e.g crude or racial comments) (Rael, 2010).

Sibona's study also suggests that people get de-friended online for things they say or do offline. While fifty-seven percent of those surveyed de-friend for online reasons, another nearly twenty-seven percent de-friend for offline behavior (Rael, 2010). Sibona also asked about the impact on the Facebook friend who is de-friended (Rael, 2010) While some people just laugh it off, others are traumatized. "There are a wide variety of reactions depending on who did the de-friending and why," says Sibona (Rael, 2010).

The Attraction to Connection

With approximately five million accounts on Facebook alone, one would assume privacy is a paramount issue (Govani & Pashley, 2005). However, it appears that members are still pulled in by the appeal of maintaining and developing new connections. In fact, Govani and Pashley (2005) point out that Facebook users join the network because of friends that are already members, to find old friend, to meet new people, and to make it easier for others to find them and keep in touch with them. While most users are friends with classmates and people from their past on such network, a majority use these networks to be connected with people they are not close with and people they do not count as friends (Govani & Pashley, 2005). Still, almost fifty percent of online social network users are connected to people they have never even met (Govani & Pashley, 2005). It is evident that people, regardless of their gender or age, and in spite of the negative aspects of online social networking, notice the benefits of connecting instantly online. Thus, they continue to use online social networks as a means for maintaining and developing friendships, relationships, and connection in general.

The arrival, and constant evolution, of the Internet and social media have played a significant role in people's lives and relationships. The infinite space of the Internet leaves plenty of room for imagination, lust, and wonder. It is that space that people try and find, fill, and discover themselves and their relationships, perhaps not realizing the extent to which it may be damaging. Despite limits to privacy and various other ramifications to online self-disclosure, the internet is proving to be a largely positive tool for creating and maintaining social relationships,. With the financials and demographics to back it up, it appears as though the positive aspects of online networking outweigh the bad.

Where will relationships evolve to next? How will our definitions and social meanings change?? Only time will tell. However one thing is certain: cyber space is affecting our lives in immeasurable ways, re-defining our perceptions of fidelity, delineating the boundaries of friendships and relationships, morphing language, and transforming the way people communicate and connect. Perhaps in the next decade will be speaking in acronyms only. Or perhaps everyone will meet their potential partners through the Internet only. Regardless of where the Internet leads us, it is leading us in a direction towards more unison, more connectedness.

References

Alexander, S. (2009, April 6). *Emotional infidelity*. Retrieved from www.womansavers.com

Barnes, S.B. (2001). *Online connections: Internet interpersonal relationships*. Cresskill, New Jersey: Hampton Press. Inc.

Cacioppo, John. (2009, July 27). Dimensions of Human Connection: People, Pets, and Prayers? Retrieved from http://psychologytoday.com.

Card, O. S. (1985). *Ender's Game*. New York: Tor Books.

Chatroulette (n.d.). In *Wikipedia*. Retrieved February 28, 2011, from http://en.wikipedia.org/wiki/Chatroulette

Coyle, C. L. & Vaughn, H. (2008). Social networking: Communication revolution or evolution? *Bell Labs Technical Journal, 13(2)*, p.13-18.

Emoticon. (n.d.). In *Wikipedia*. Retrieved February 28, 2011, from http://en.wikipedia.org/wiki/Emoticon

Epstein, R. (2009). The Truth about Online Dating. Scientific American Mind, 20(3), 54-61. Retrieved from EBSCOhost

Govani, T. & Pashley, H. (2005). Student awareness of the privacy implications when using Facebook. Unpublished manuscript retrieved from http://lorrie.cranor.org/courses/fa05/tubzhlp.pdf.

Hargittai, E. (2007). Whose space? Differences among users and non-users of social network sites. *Journal of Computer-Mediated Communication, 13*(1), article 14. Retrieved from: http://jcmc.indiana.edu/vol13/issue1/hargittai.html.

Helsper, E. J. (2010). Gendered Internet use across generations and life stages. *Communication Research, 37*(3), p. 352-374.

Hartley, S. (2008). *Extramarital dating.* Retrieved from www. illicitencounters.com

Houston, R. (2006, May 7). *The truth about cyber affairs.* Retrieved from http://www.authorsden.com/visit/viewarticle.asp?AuthorID=9889&id=22092

Jaffe, A. (2010, April 17). Facebook, e-mail, games, and porn—A glimpse at our addiction to technology. *Psychology Today.* Retrieved from http://www.psychologytoday.com/blog/all-about-addiction

Kalish, N. (2009, September 17). Extramarital affairs in the new millennium. *Psychology*

Today. Retrieved from http://www.psychologytoday.com/blog/sticky-bonds/200909/extramarital-affairs-in-the-new-millennium

Muise, A., Christofides, E., & Desmaraise, S. (2009). More information than you ever wanted: Does Facebook bring out the green-eyed monster of jealousy? *Cyber Psychology & Behavior, 12*(4), p. 441-444.

North, S. (2007). "The voices, the voices": Creativity in online conversation. *Applied Linguistics, 28(4),* p.538-555.

Parks, M. & Roberts, L. (1998). "Making MOOsic": The development of personal relationships online and a comparison to their off-line counterparts. *Journal of Social and Personal Relationships, 15*(4), p.517-537.

Paolillo, J. C. (2001). Language variation on Internet relay chat: A social network approach. *Journal of Sociolinguistics,* 5(2), p.180-213.

Paolillo, J. (1999). The virtual speech community: Social network and language variation. *Journal of Computer-Mediated Communication, 4(4),* DOI: 10.1111/j.1083-6101.

Parsons, J. M. (2005). An Examination of massively multiplayer online role-playing games as a facilitator of internet addiction. Retrieved from http://ir.uiowa.edu/etd/98

Rael, A. (2010, October 5). CU-Denver student examines the reasons for Facebook unfriending. *The Huffington Post*. Retrieved from google. cohttp://www.huffingtonpost.com/2010/10/05/unmasking-the-reasons-beh_n_751269.html

Rimskii, V. (2010). The Influence of the Internet on Active Social Involvement and the Formation and Development of Identities. Russian Education & Society, 52(8), 11-33. doi:10.2753/RES1060-9393520802

Sheeks, M.S., & Birchmeier, Z.P. (2007). Shyness, sociability, and the use of computer-mediated communication in relationship development. *Cyber Psychology and Behavior, 10* (1), p. 64-70.

Squires, L. (2010). Enregistering internet language. Language in Society, 39(4), 457-492. Doi:10.1017/S0047404510000412

Stephure, R. J., Boon, S. D., MacKinnon, S. L., & Deveau, V. L. (2009). Internet initiated relationships: Associations between age and involvement in online dating. *Computer-Mediated Communication, 14*(3), p. 658-681.

Walther, J. B., Van Der Heide, B., Kim, S., Westerman, D., & Tong, S. T. (2008.) The role of friends' appearance and behavior on evaluations of individuals on Facebook: Are we known by the company we keep? *Human Communication Research, 34*(1), p. 28-49.

Wildermuth, S. M. & Vogl-Bauer, S. (2007). We met on the net: Exploring the perceptions of online romantic relationship participants. *Southern Communication Journal, 72(3)*, p.211-227.

Wu, P. & Chiou, W. (2009). Rapid communication: More options lead to more searching and worse choices in finding partners for romantic relationships online: An experimental study. *Cyber Psychology & Behavior, 12(3)*, p.315-318.

CHAPTER 2

Adolescents,
the Internet, and Sexuality

Andrea Castro
Meredith Hartin
Gina Kamnit
Marina Voron

For today's youth, access to the Internet is a right, not a privilege. Gone are the days of traveling to public libraries or Internet cafés to check one's e-mail. Aside from one's home computer, adolescents can gain access to the Internet through laptops, cell phones, and iPods. These mobile devices allow for 24 hours a day, seven days a week access to Internet material. As the Internet has become available through such a wide variety of portals, parents are less able to monitor and restrict the online activities of their children. As the next wave of children enter adolescence, it is important to examine the impact of such technological advances on their sexual development and behavior.5

Teenagers utilize the Internet for a variety of purposes, both for education and entertainment. These include school-related research, social networking, gathering information about personal interests, and playing video games. Currently in the United States, social networking sites, such as Facebook, MySpace, and Twitter, are a primary form of communication and social interaction amongst teens. Online video games, such as the "massively multiplayer online role-playing games" (Griffiths, Davies, & Chappell, 2004, p. 88) allow players to create a character that represents them as they explore their online gaming world and engage in text chats with others. These forums enable participants to interact with thousands of players across the globe. As Borzekowski and Rickert (2001) discovered, adolescents are looking to access health information online as well. They found adolescents' most frequently searched health topics to be "health risk behaviors," such as unprotected sex and physical or sexual abuse. Today's teenagers seem to be having increasingly common experiences with these issues, as they are seeking information for a reason.

Historical Adolescent Development and Socialization

What defines adolescence is constantly changing as time goes on. The extended period between childhood and adulthood, mainly due to increases in education, is a new historical period in social development. "What we know about the extension of schooling supports the supposition that entrance into adulthood has been delayed" (Model, Furstenburg, & Hershberg, 1976, Timing section, para. 2). This is now the period of time in which adolescents begin to develop their identities and begin to improve their cognitive abilities and socialization skills.

Muuss (1988) presents the idea of systems in which this process of adolescent socialization develops. Three of the systems include the microsystem, mesosystem, and exosystem. The microsystem includes the small units in an adolescent's life, such as family and place of school. The mesosystem incorporates the relationships between the small sub-units. For example, the values that one's family instills will affect the way an adolescent behaves within the schooling system, and thus will affect the type of peer that they choose to, or want to socialize with. The exosystem consists of the large systems that exist outside the adolescent's community that play an effect on all systems, such as trends and ideas popularized by mass media. (p.302-305). All of these systems have an impact on the adolescent. Maneuvering throughout the relationships of these systems while making the attempts to form new peer groups that will in turn interact and become another subgroup takes a great deal of cognitive ability. "For each individual adolescent, a continuously interacting set of complex social relationships exists" (Muuss, 1988, p.301). Within these social relationships, roles are allocated and positions are identified. Friendship and group support are an integral part of these negotiations.

During this transition between childhood and adulthood there is rapid biological and cognitive growth. This has an effect on the child's view of themselves and the systems that surround them. Puberty is beginning, self definition is occurring, and the transition to a more independent stage in life is starting. An important piece of this transition is peer group identification. This new social learning sets the wheel in motion as to how these adolescents will socialize, and where they will place themselves in the interrelated systems as adults.

Peer group association is an integral part of this life transition. The first step in coming to decisions about peer group affiliations is gaining independence from the parental microsystem. Berndt (1982) in his studies of theories of adolescence remarked about this significant transformation in relationships. (p.1447). The new autonomy gives rise to new experiences of choice. This occurs at a similar time to when adolescents are more apt to understand cognitively whom they want to associate themselves with and with whom they can recognize and reciprocate more meaningful relationships with.

Researchers agree that the basis to peer group formation initially entails a group of individuals that are similar in a variety of ways that unite them. "Early adolescents sometimes are described as choosing friends with complimentary interests and traits, friends whom they can idealize or friends who engage in behaviors that fascinate them but are afraid to perform themselves" (Berndt, 1982, p.1453). Often socio-economic subsystems or religion will form a peer group due not to mindful choices, but due to convenience and similarity. As autonomy is further placed as preference in the adolescents mind though, they are able to make choices as whether to continue to solidify these convenient peer groups, or explore new ones that differ from experiences they have had in the past.

Historically, choice of friends have been limited by microsystems such as families, and those families' relationships within the mesosystem, such as how they relate to the schools in the area, the churches, the local neighborhood. Within the limits of geographic location, transportation, and communication technology, friends were chosen to comprise peer groups. These groups were convenient to the technology and the relationships of the time.

What is different about the chosen friends of adolescence and those of childhood are the level that the friendships are understood at. "Most theorists have assumed that intimate relationships first emerge during adolescence . . . intimate relationships only are possible when children reach a certain level of role taking ability" (Berndt, 1982, p.1448). This intimacy is one that describes a level of friendship that is understood by both parties in the dyad. Both sides in this deeper friendship will understand the likes and dislikes of the other, the effect they have on the other, the reciprocity of actions, and so forth. This mutual understanding continues to develop throughout newly formed friendships as well as can be applied to past ones. The ability to cognitively process ones role in the friendship is a sign of the advancement in socialization skills acquired during the adolescent period. The ability to choose friends and understand the dynamics is an important developmental skill.

The ability to cognitively process friendships on deeper levels is only one of the myriads of benefits that friends and more advanced peer groups have on adolescents. "Group belonging provides young people with a sense of definition, purpose, meaning, worth, and social control, all of which contribute to mental health" (Newman, Lohman, and Philip, 2007, p.259). By being able to disassociate with the identity of themselves in parental definitions and begin to develop their own definitions of themselves in relation to their new peer group, the adolescent is newly empowered by their independence. This empowerment and autonomy has a positive correlation with self-esteem. Within his studies with singular best friends, Berndt (1982) found that those with a close and stable best friend had higher self-esteem than did those that did not. (p.1450). Establishing a close network of chosen peers affords adolescents the ability to maintain and choose those friends within the group that they most closely want to relate to.

Reciprocity is a skill that is continuously developing as one ages. The ability to understand the positive or negative aspects of a behavior and respond with a behavior that has the same affect on the other person is important when relating to different peers. "With increases in their cognitive abilities adolescents become more capable of sharing their thoughts and feelings with friends; they also acquire a more mature understanding of reciprocity and equality in friendships" (Berndt, 1982, p.1457). No longer will parents, teachers, club organizers, or other guiding figures hold together peer groups and provide a grounds for understanding of the friendships within those groups. Adolescents, now cognitively able, are responsible for their own actions and are able to recognize their behaviors affect on others and on themselves.

The benefits of organizing and maintaining these peer groups extend beyond the adolescent stage. They are a basis for future socialization skills. Peer group association provides a basis for social reinforcement. "The focal adolescent goes along with behavioral suggestions of friends or peers for the sake of the social reinforcement (in terms of status, praise, recognition, or group admiration received in return" (Muuss, 1988, p.317). Adolescents learn what is acceptable and valued among their peer grounds and then must actively decide how those behaviors can benefit their own selves. If deemed good and acceptable, these positive behaviors will be reinforced and esteem garnered by the group will be raised.

These positive value exchanges are important for future adult relationships. "Interactions with friends can serve as a foundation for egalitarian relationships with colleagues, neighbors or spouses in adulthood" (Berndt, 1982, p.1448). If socialization skills are not honed in adolescent it can become difficult to form the necessary relationships in adulthood that have the potential to lead to successes and happiness. The difficulties in socializing, if not addressed early, may continue to repeat themselves leading to unacceptable behaviors or mental negativity.

It is not only future concerns, but the inability to maintain friendships and peer group affiliations have an immediate effect on the adolescent as well. "Lack of a sense of peer group belonging places the adolescence at a greater risk for both internalizing and externalizing problems than does peer group membership" (Newman, Lohman, and Newman, 2007, p 245). Peers provide a means for the adolescents to express themselves. They also relay a feeling of acceptance and relatedness. By being able to express their feelings within an accepting group the adolescent is able to vent frustrations and concerns knowing that they will be supported. They also gain a positive sense of self when they are able to understand and accept one of their peers in a time of needed expression.

Increases in behavior problems are noticed among adolescents as the desire for social acceptance is increased. "Feelings of social distress are greatest for those adolescents who strongly desire group membership and do not experience a sense of group belonging" (Newman, Lohman, and Newman, p.243). The feelings of social distress have a positive correlation with acting out behaviors. Often, these rebellious acts are intended to gain the attention of the desired group, but display that the individual has not developed the socialization skills that garner positive social reinforcement. Often these negative behaviors are co-morbid with depression and anxiety.

The period of adolescence has become an integral part of the lifelong social learning process. With both positive and negative affects for the individual, it is fundamental that the peer group affiliation and friendship recognition be nurtured. This learning process can aid in developing the skills needed for future correspondence and even future romantic relationships.

Historical Adolescent Relationship Development

Adolescence can be a very difficult period during an individual's life. There are many changes that individuals in this stage go through, such as physical and emotional changes. During the adolescence stage, individuals are faced with a series of developmental tasks that should be completed before they enter into the next life cycle stage. The main theme of this stage is becoming an individual separate from their family of origin. At this time, adolescents must begin to alter the relationships that they have with their family members, allowing themselves to become more autonomous (Furman and Shaffer, 2003). As well, they must begin to form relationships with their peers, outside of their family of origin.

There are also changes occurring among peer groups and the types of relationships that they have. Teenagers at this time are developing sexually; therefore certain relationships with other individuals begin to change. Prior to this stage, friendships have been typically formed based on gender. Maccoby (1998) stated that it was not until early or middle adolescence that adolescents begin to interact with members of the opposite sex in group settings (as cited in O'Sullivan, Cheng, Harris and Brooks-Gunn, 2007, p. 100). Once individuals reach this stage, they begin to notice an increased interested in the opposite sex. Males and females begin to look at members of the opposite sex as whether or not they could form a romantic relationship or just maintain a friendship (Furman and Wehner, 1997). Brown (1999) stated similar findings that adolescents begin looking to members of the opposite sex as potential romantic and/ or sexual partners.

Relationships that occur early on in the adolescent stage have been socially referred to as "puppy love" due to its casual nature. Brown (1999) referred to this point as the initiation phase, which he defined as a turning point where the adolescent becomes involved romantically with members of the opposite sex. At this time, there is an increased interest in sexual expression and romantic relationships. Relationships during this time are not very serious; in fact relationships tend to be very casual and short-lived. It is not until later on that a romantic partner becomes more than just a companion. Partners during this time usually do not turn to each other for support; instead, individuals turn to their friends to provide them with this. One study showed that romantic activity in this age group was very low and the duration of the relationship was very short compared to the other age groups seen in the study (Seiffge-Krenke, 2003).

Even though, the relationships are not exclusive or as serious as adult relationships, the development of romantic relationships remains to be a central issue for teenagers (Furman & Shaffer, 2003). Among adolescent peer groups, usually the topic of conversation remains on romantic relationships. The importance of romantic relationships is so great that according to Wilson-Shockley (1995), real and fantasized relationships among adolescents were the most common cause of eliciting strong positive and negative emotions (as cited in Furman & Shaffer, 2003, p. 3).

Peer groups play a very vital role in the development of a relationship. Friends will turn to each other for advice on who to date. As well, before starting a romantic relationship with another person, individuals look to their friends for approval. Early relationships during this stage are focused primarily on finding a partner that will help increase their status among their peers (Brown, 1999). Simon, Aikins and Prinstein (2008), found that status grading is an important part of a relationship. There is much focus on who it is they are dating, whether the individual is attractive and there is much influence from their peers (Furman and Wehner, 1997). Teenagers choose their partners depending on the approval from their friends. Friends begin to play the role of judges, encouraging each other on whom to date. Interestingly enough, adolescent relationships are usually formed in peer groups (Simon, Aikins, and Prinstein, 2008).

As adolescents begin to move forward in this life cycle stage, romantic relationships as well begin to evolve. In what Brown (1999) refers to as the affection phase, the partners become more involved romantically and the focus begins to move away from the self and more towards the couple. Peer groups during this phase begin to have less of an impact on the relationship. As individuals during this point progress throughout the stage, romantic relationships begin to focus less on their peer groups and become more sexual in nature (Meier and Allen, 2009). Partners begin to form a companionship and become more emotionally supportive of each other.

In the final stage, the bonding phase, individuals become committed in the relationship and the possibility of staying together forever becomes a concern during this phase (as cited in Seiffge-Krenke, 2003, p. 520). The romantic relationship at this point has more of an importance than it did in the past. Romantic partners begin to become the main focus and replace the role that peer groups used to play.

Types of Romantic Relationships

As was stated in the previous section, romantic relationships are a big part of the adolescent life. Relationships are the main topic of conversation among individuals. Conversations usually include speaking about who is dating who, the progression of the relationship and/or an argument that the two partners might have had. As a result, there are many different types of relationships and meanings that teenagers attach to them. Romantic relationships at this time can range from a casual relationship, dating more than one partner or a steady relationship. Davis and Windle (2000) in their study stated that adolescent relationships fit four different relationship patterns. The different patterns included: 1) no dating relationships; 2) a single, casual dating relationship; 3) multiple, casual relationships 4) steady dating relationships (as cited in Meier and Allen, 2009, p. 311).

Another type of relationship that appears to be prevalent among teenagers is what many call "friends with benefits." These types of relationships are a combination of a typical friendship and a romantic relationship. Individuals in these relationships "are not romantically committed and do not share a romantic love for one another", however they "engage in repeated sexual activity" (Bisson & Levine, 2009, p. 67). "Friends with benefits" relationships are described as having the characteristics of a friendship while avoiding the romance aspect of romantic relationships (Hughes, Morrison & Asada, 2005). When comparing the differences between a friendship and a romantic relationship, one can see that there are many differences between the two. Unlike close friendships, romantic relationships tend to be shorter in duration and there is the issue of being exclusive with each other. While individuals tend to become friends with others who share similarities, romantic partners do not share many commonalities. Also, with romantic partners there exists in communication a sort of awkwardness between the individuals (Giordano, 2006).

Benefits of Adolescent Romantic Relationships

According to the Teenage Research Unlimited (2006), statistics show that one half of adolescents stated that they have been in a romantic relationship. One third of these respondents described their relationship as being a serious one (as cited in Sorensen, 2007, p. 1). Therefore, since there are large amounts of teenagers dating and probably even more are interested in dating, it is important to explore the possible benefits and detriments that may come as a result of being in a romantic relationship.

Let's first take a look at the benefits that come with being in a healthy romantic relationship. Healthy relationships are described as ones which have open communication and high levels of trust. Healthy relationships aid adolescents to complete certain developmental tasks such as forming a sense of identity. Relationships in general can help them gain a "greater understanding of who they are and what they value" (Sorensen, 2007, p. 2). Romantic relationships can also improve interpersonal skills, such as improving communication and negotiation skills and developing empathy. The development of these skills serves to be beneficial with other relationships that adolescents may have in the future (Sorensen, 2007).

Detriments of Adolescent Romantic Relationships

While adolescent romantic relationship has many benefits, there are many detriments that may come with dating. Silverman, Raj, Mucci and Hathaway (2001) found that "one fifth of adolescent women are victims of physical or sexual abuse by a dating partner" (as cited in Furman, 2002, p. 178). Domestic violence is a very serious issue that for young individuals to experience can be detrimental. Due to their lack of dating experience, teenagers may not be prepared to deal with the violence or they may fear turning to an adult for help; therefore staying in the situation. According to the Centers for Disease Control and Prevention (2009), one out of every 10 high school students (9.8%) was a victim of dating violence in 2009, with 9% of girls reporting having been hit, slapped, or physically hurt by a romantic partner in the 12 months preceding the survey, and 10% of boys reporting the same (as cited in ACT for Youth Center of Excellence, 2010, p. 3). According to Teenage Research Unlimited (2006) about 61% of adolescents have been in a relationship in which a partner has put them down or humiliated them (as cited in Sorensen, 2007, p. 2).

The increase of sexuality among adolescents can also prove to be detrimental to individuals at this stage. Teenagers, who are involved in romantic relationships, may begin to have sexual intercourse with their partners. Teenage Research Unlimited (2006), found that "one out of four teens report having sex is expected if you are in a relationship and almost one-third of teen girls who had been in a relationship said that they have been pressured to have sex or engage in sexual acts when they did not want to" (as cited in Sorensen, 2007, p. 2). These sexual acts put teenagers at risk for sexually transmitted infections (STIs) and increase the chances of teenage pregnancy (Furman, 2002).

The Internet

Statistics: Social Networking Sites

The Internet is having a significant impact on the way that lives are being lived. For many adults the idea of online social networking is an adjustment. For today's teens it is part of their everyday lives. Statistics on the rise of Internet use display the popularity and normalization of this new medium for socialization.

There are numerous networking sites that exist. It seems as if there are categories to fit almost anyone's interest, from the animal lover to the avid hunter. Many of these sites do though have an age requirement for users. The most popular sites for the thirteen and up crowd seem to be Bebo, MySpace, Habbo, and Facebook. They are the most easily accessible through Internet search engines. The popularity of these sites tend to ebb and flow, but the most popular sites are representative of the overall normalization of this new form of communication, socialization, and peer group formation.

The Pew Internet and American Life Project (2000) took a national sample of 12-17 year olds to analyze their Internet usage. According to their findings, 55% of online teens created their own personal profiles. 48% of those visit those profiles daily. The information revealed on these websites can be personal, but studies seem to show that teens are aware in some part about keeping certain information private. A quantitative analysis of MySpace conducted by Hinduja and Patchen (2007) discovered that while 40% of those in their study revealed their first names, only 9% revealed their full names. Although their findings also uncovered that 81% revealed their current city, 28% their current school, and 57% had a photo of the teen, many personal profiles could not be analyzed because they were set to private. (p.127). These privacy settings allow only accepted users be able to view the contents of their profiles.

The use of personal profiles and online socialization seems to be skyrocketing according to Facebook statistics alone. According to their website, Facebook (2010) opened it registration process to high school networks in 2005. Shortly after, it was opened to the general public. Since allowing a greater population of users to register, anyone thirteen or older, Facebook boasts that they have 500 million users. Of those 500 million users, 50% will log on at any given day. The average user has 130 friends and will spend over 700 minutes per month on their site. Because of privacy regulations, Facebook does not break down their users into specific criterion, but it is fair to assume that a large percentage of their users are in the teenage age range. They are the most comfortable and natural users of sites such as Facebook.

For teenage Americans, the use of the Internet as a source of normal socialization is common. The Pew Internet (2000) survey also revealed that 91% of online teens use the Internet and social networking sites to stay in touch with friends and 72% use it to make plans with friends. Most of these friends that they correspond with online are ones who were previously gained through Microsystems such as school. Instant messaging programs and e-mail make staying in touch and making plans convenient for the teens.

Statistics: Instant Messaging and E-Mail

The Pew Internet and American Life Project (2000) conducted another study on teenage internet usage that revealed that 74% of online teens used instant messaging. It seems for teens to be a convenient way to stay in touch with multiple friends simultaneously while also being able to do other tasks. Telephone limits what the teenager is able to do as well as limits the amount of friends they can stay in touch with a certain time period.

Another option teens employed to keep up with their communication is e-mail. A study conducted by Schiano et al. (c.2001) revealed that most teenagers checked their e-mails at least once a night. (Results and Discussion section para. 1). For a fair percentage of teens checking e-mail coincides with instant messaging and perusing their friends personal profile pages. Communication options seem to be at their fingertips whenever they choose to use it.

As technology increases, the ability to multi task between communication options online increases. Also, the ability to bring these options outside of the home is presently increasing as well due to the new influx of smartphones equipped with internet capabilities. The Schiano et. Al (c.2001) study of teens media messaging usage predicts that the ownership of mobile phones is soon to reach 85% of the population before they reach the age of 18. (Introduction section, para. 2). With the current trend in internet ready phones, it seems that this soon to be 85% will not have to be without socialization options including e-mail and instant messaging. It is more and more convenient to put this technology in a pocket to utilize it whenever it is convenient.

Statistics: Adolescent Dating

The Internet has been widely used by many individuals, for example, almost 93% of teenagers between the ages of 12 and 17 utilize the internet (Lenhart, Purcell, Smith & Zickuhr, 2010). For individuals this age, the internet serves many purposes, including an educational and communication tool. The internet is used to connect with other individuals, mostly of similar ages, while using social networking sites such as Facebook and Myspace. It was found that 73% of teenagers between the ages of 12 and 17 were part of a social networking site (Lenhart et al., 2010). These social networking sites, allow individuals to become acquainted with others of similar interests. As well, they are used to maintain current romantic relationships through the use of leaving wall posts for a romantic partner. Adolescents can also use their profiles to tell the world who they are currently dating.

According to Wolak et al. (2002), about 2% of adolescents interviewed in the study had developed a romantic relationship online. Most of these individuals were between the ages of 14 and 17. About 28% of these individuals also reported meeting their romantic partner that they met online. The researchers in addition found that about 83% of these individuals became involved romantically with someone who was either the same age or a year older. Online chat rooms are used frequently by individuals to search for potential romantic partners. Smahel and Subrahmanyam (2007) found that teenagers use these rooms to find potential partners by asking members of the chat room to press 123, for example, if anyone is interested in chatting (Subrahmanyam & Greenfield, 2008, p. 129).

The internet and other technological devices, such as cellular phones have been used to connect with a person's boyfriend or girlfriend. According to a survey by Teenage Research unlimited, about 25% of teenagers in a romantic relationship have used a cell phone or texting their partners (as cited in Subrahmanyam & Greenfield, 2008, p. 129). Bryant et al. (2006) found that among the seventh grade students that were surveyed 24% of them had used the instant messaging to break up with their partner.

Joan D. Atwood, Ph.D., LMFT, LCSW & Conchetta Gallo, Ph.D., LMFT

Social Networking Sites

Children are being drawn into the world of online social networking at younger ages with the development of ClubPenguin and Webkins (Delmonico & Griffin, 2008). These sites allow users to engage with peers in an online community via their "pets." As these children come of age, they will likely transition to the mainstream social networking sites. Hundreds of millions of individuals are accessing these websites on a consistent basis. Facebook reports having more than 500 million active users, with over 200 million users accessing the application through their mobile devices (Facebook, 2010). MySpace boasts having more than 100 million users worldwide (MySpace, 2010), which is surprisingly modest in comparison to Facebook. Twitter reports having 175 million registered users (Twitter, 2010), a fair start for the newest addition. As technology continues to develop, users no longer need a computer to access these websites. All three of these social networking sites have created mobile applications for cell phones and iPods, allowing members to update their statuses and "tweet" anytime, anywhere.

While these sites are intended to promote socialization and networking, they have also been utilized as forums for sexual activity and discussion. Social networking sites provide users the opportunity to post pictures of themselves, as well as their friends, and then link friends' pages to the pictures by "tagging" them. Frequently, adolescents are posting sexualized pictures of themselves, despite these sites allowing for public access. In a study of undergraduate students, Peluchette and Karl (2008) found that "males were significantly more likely than females to place self-promoting and risqué pictures or comments (involving sex or alcohol) on their profile" (p. 96). As this study involved a self-report questionnaire, it is possible females found it less socially desirable to admit posting sexually provocative photographs of themselves. Moreno, VanderStoep, Parks, Zimmerman, Kurth, and Christakis (2009) found that "displaying sexual behavior references on a popular adolescent Web site [such as Facebook, MySpace, or Twitter] may increase pressure to become sexually active among virginal adolescents" (p. 39). These findings suggest that simply observing a peer being portrayed in a sexualized manner can influence an adolescent's sexuality.

Internet Pornography

In addition to social networking websites, the Internet provides virtually unlimited access to various forms of pornography. Finkelhor, Mitchell, and Wolak (2000) report that 25 percent of American teenagers who regularly use the Internet encounter unwanted pornography. Such statistics suggest that even those adolescents who are not actively looking for sexual material online may encounter it at some point. Many others, however, are actively searching. "Sex" is one of the most frequently searched for words on the Internet (Freeman-Longo, 2000). Cooper (2000) reports that sales related to sex on the Internet are the third largest economic category on the Internet. The ease with which adolescents may access Internet material poses an important question—how is the increased availability of pornography affecting adolescent sexuality? Such access is providing youth with opportunities to seek out sexual and romantic partners, as well as entertainment through sexual material on the Internet (Boies, 2002).

Carnes (2001) presents the concept of the "arousal template," or a set of sexual preferences first established during childhood. This set can be adapted and influenced according to one's life experiences. He suggests that certain paraphilias are created in this way. Brown (2000) suggests that adolescents' exposure to sexual media content reinforces a particular set of sexual and relational norms, as well as sexually irresponsible behavior. One may conclude that if Internet pornography is portraying sex and sexuality in an aggressive, idealistic, or extreme way, viewers may be led to believe such experiences are "the norm." Adolescents may internalize unrealistic expectations in regards to sex, thus significantly impacting their sexual development and future relationships. Clearly, exposure to pornography has the potential to shape one's sexual development. The ease with which such material may be accessed by today's teenagers is concerning.

The Internet and Socialization

Adolescents will naturally begin the socialization process in schools and other organizations. The Internet though, has provided a new means by which this social learning process can continue or even where it may begin before spilling over into the outside microgroup. "Many adolescents spend hours of their day, both in school and after school, tending to their group connections. Their peer group work can be documented in note passing, e-mails, phone calls, instant messaging, during and after school talking, planning, 'hanging out' . . ." (Newman, Lohman, and Newman, 2007, p.259). With or without the internet there will be a form of socialization occurring in this life stage.

A fair amount of Internet socialization mimics real life scenarios. Hinduja and Patchin (2007) find these similarities in their studies, stating that "an Internet based social network can accordingly be considered a virtual community, consisting of characteristics displayed in real life" (128). If friends within this virtual community are not already friends in the real life community, the characteristics of these individuals will most likely be similar to the real life friends.

This mirror to real life socialization allows the adolescent to explore their social needs for more hours in the day than they previously had been able to. Also, since a fair amount of their socialization skills are refined the Internet, they are able to hone their social skills and explore their own role within their peer groups in different and more private ways. "Youth actively explore and question various beliefs, boundaries, goals and roles before assimilating those that provide a sense of uniqueness . . . this process can aptly unfold in cyberspace due to the anonymity, flexibility, and accessibility that the internet provides" (Hinduja and Patchen, 2007, p.128). Boundaries and roles are now able to be tested in person and online, giving more opportunity for self exploration to occur.

Historically as the period of adolescence lengthened, the social skills involved in identifying oneself within a peer group and as an individual entity separate from their family of origin. The new use of the Internet provides more resources for private discovery while also cementing theories of the importance of peer group development. "The work of establishing a sense of peer group interaction is evidence of a variety of healthy coping skills, including problem solving, effective communication, and emotional regulation" (Newman, Lohman, and Newman, 2007, p.259). Self identification and advance peer group building and maintenance are skill developed both online and off, as well as skills that can be utilized in both settings as well, as long as the adherence to the view that the online community is an extension of the real world community.

Although, vaguely a mirrored image of adolescents current community, the maintenance of peer groups and friendships has the opportunity to lead to stress due to the public nature of many social networking sites.

even if the privacy of communicating in the online realm, as Shiano et al. (c.2001) point out, helps some shy adolescents overcome fears and interact in more productive ways than they may in person, a new pressure to build "cultural currency" is built. The social network provides and in-depth look into ones social life. How many friends one has, how many comments others have left, and even how many pictures they have of themselves and their peers engaging in enjoyable activities and what those activities are now play a role.

The once shy, now outgoing online adolescent must make the decision to extend their role in the real world or not. They must navigate their values and need for peer acceptance, just as they would in true life. Today's adolescent can now view the impact their socialization has on their online community in comparison to their peers.

The negative aspects that social networking provide for the adolescent is similar to those experienced in real life. The want to join a particular peer group or any peer group may cause depression or anxiety. The behaviors that lead to exclusion from a peer group may be felt even more so as it is able to be witnessed by the excluded individual outside of the normal peer environment. They can now experience their seclusion at almost any time in their online environment. Bullying and peer pressures already felt in real life environments can now extend to online communities wherein anonymity may increase the amount by which one bullies due to the anonymity the Internet provides. This in turn may extend anxieties and depressions related to bullying circumstances beyond the parameters experienced by youth in the past.

Like every new change in the way people socialize, there are positives and negatives. What is important to focus on though is the lessons one can learn as they develop new friendships and peer groups. Positive behavior, reciprocity, and understanding the affect as an individual within a dyad or a group, will be skills that can be taken and applied in this new medium as well as traditional mediums as youth grow and venture into new and more mature relationships.

The Internet and Romantic Relationships

Technology today has affected tremendously the way teenagers interact with each other. Instant messengers, text messages and email have increasingly become the main ways in which teenagers communicate.

According to Lenhart, Rainie & Lewis (2001), the most used tool among adolescents is instant messaging. About 74% of adolescents use this form of technology to communicate with their friends. IMs are being used more and more as a way of maintaining relationships (as cited in Bryant, Sanders-Jackson & Smallwood, 2006, p. 579). "Adolescents appear to use electronic media to reinforce existing romantic relationships, just as they do friendships" (Subrahmanyam & Greenfield, 2008, p. 128).

The internet has changed the way romantic relationships are formed. As stated previously, there are many stages in the development of a relationship which has since been affected by the internet. The way individuals relate to each other during face to face interactions is quite different compared to interactions done online. The awkwardness that comes with meeting a member of the opposite sex and all the worries that come with these interactions are removed when using the internet. Many teenagers find it easier to relate to others online, since there is no need to worry about physical appearance or awkward silences and not knowing what to say next. One study found that adolescents, who may have trouble forming friendships as a result of shyness, seem to turn to the internet to form relationships (Mesch, 2001). According to Derlega and Chaikin (1977), individuals forming relationships are usually wary of disclosing information. Partners tend not to share information until they feel they have trust in the relationship (as cited in McKenna, Green, and Gleason, 2002, p. 10).

The impact of the internet on how individuals socialize with each other has become a topic of debate among researchers. Increasingly, teenagers have become more and more dependent on communicating using the internet and text messages. The increased usage of these resources, according to some researchers, has affected the way they interact. There is less time being spent having a normal face-to-face interaction, which in turn causes relationships with their family and friends to weaken (Lee, 2009).

Arrival of the Internet

Since its arrival, the internet has been connecting together individuals from all over the world. The internet, at first, became an important tool for education; however it has now grown into communication tool (Subrahmanyam & Greenfield, 2008). According to Wellman and Gulia

(1998), the internet has become primarily used for communicating with others. Many use the internet to communicate with former and current friends, create new relationships and for social support (as cited in Mesch, 2001, p. 329). Adolescents, for example, have become the biggest group to use the internet for connecting with other individuals, who are of the same age.

Adolescents primarily have turned to the web for pursuing relationships. One study found that Internet users between the ages of 10 and 17 turned to the internet to communicate with other individuals (Wolak, Mitchell & Finkelhor, 2002).

Adolescents, especially, have been the most attracted to social networks such as Facebook and MySpace, among others. Perhaps its attractiveness is linked to the feeling of remaining anonymous even while interacting with other individuals. Kling (1996) argued that the internet is an attractive tool for adolescents, who may have trouble socializing during face-to-face interactions (as cited in Mesch, 2001, p. 330). Talking online eases the feelings of being self-conscious of being judged and allows adolescents to plan what they will say next during the conversation (Wolak et al., 2002). In one study, researchers found that adolescents with poor interpersonal relationships were at a high risk for problematic internet use (Milani, Osualdella & Di Blasio, 2009). Mesch (2003) found that individuals who used the internet frequently reported lower levels of attachment to close friends. As well, findings showed that the frequency of internet use among adolescents affected their perceptions about the quality of family relationships (as cited in Subrahmanyam & Lin, 2007, p. 660).

By turning to the internet, adolescents are able to form new relationships with individuals that they never met before. According to Parks and Floyd (1996), in their study on a newsgroup, about two thirds of the individuals stated that they had formed a personal relationship with someone that they met online (as cited in Mesch, 2001, p. 331). According to a study done by Wolak et al. (2002), about 55% of the young adults that they interviewed used chat rooms, instant messages, e-mail and other forms of communications to interact with a person that they did not know personally. In this same study, 14% of these individuals reported that they developed a close friendship online, 7% had an in-person meeting with someone they met online and 2% developed a romantic relationship. Gross et al. (2002) found that adolescents who had reported feeling lonely or socially anxious on a certain day would turn to communicating with unknown individuals online (as cited in Subrahmanyam & Lin, 2007, p. 661).

Adolescents, the Internet, and Cybersex

Cybersex may be defined as "the pursuit of sexual interests online" (Cooper, Delmonico, & Burg, 2000, p. 6). This concept encompasses a wide variety of activities, including accessing Internet pornography, engaging in sexual conversations with online peers, and utilizing webcams while performing sexual acts. Perhaps the more "traditional" idea of cybersex involves two individuals expressing their sexual desires via a text chat online. With various technological developments, the world of cybersex has expanded. Since webcams have become available, they have been "used by teens to experiment with seductive, voyeuristic, and exhibitionistic sexual behaviors that were not as readily available prior to [their] availability" (Delmonico & Griffin, 2008, p.432). Again, as technology continues to advance, adolescents can explore new and different ways to express their sexuality.

Cooper (1998) identified the "Triple-A Engine," or three characteristics of the Internet that perpetuate sexual behavior. These include accessibility, affordability, and anonymity. In the United States, approximately 240 million people were using the Internet in 2007 (Computer Industry Almanac, 2007). Such statistics certainly speak to the Internet's accessibility. If a family were unable to afford the monthly payment for Internet access in their home, free wireless access is available at a variety of popular businesses and libraries. Once in the online realm, one's name, age, and other personal characteristics become non-existent and identities are formed around text communications and simulated characters. The Triple-A Engine has been found to increase the opportunity for individuals with pre-existing sexually compulsive behavior to escalate into addiction or other sexual issues (Cooper, Delmonico, & Burg, 2000). With almost 70 million people engaging in cybersex (Goldberg, Peterson, Rosen, & Sara, 2008), these characteristics have clearly had an impact.

Benefits of Cybersex

There are benefits to engaging in cybersex, rather than in-person sexual intercourse. The risks of unplanned pregnancy, contracting sexually transmitted diseases and infections, and physical harm are virtually eliminated, providing the sexual partners do not meet in real-life. If implemented with knowledge and care, cybersex may be a healthy alternative for virginal adolescents. Cooper, McLoughlin, and Campbell (2000) propose that the development of romantic relationships online allows for them to be based on "emotional intimacy rather than lustful attraction" (p. 522), as one's physical attributes are unknown. It provides the opportunity for partners to get to know one another in an intimate, emotional way prior to evaluating one another on physical attractiveness. Additional benefits include the opportunity to "reduce limitations of gender roles; allow each partner to feel autonomous within the relationship; encourage open, intimate, and direct communication; and provide a safe environment for the inexperienced to practice flirtation and experimentation with different sex roles and personas" (p. 522). Again, such benefits may be accessed when cybersex is engaged in safely and with proper precautions.

Associated Risks

Various risks are associated with adolescents' increased use of the Internet for sexual purposes, including victimization by others and the development of "unhealthy sexual behavior patterns" (Delmonico & Griffin, 2008, p. 431). Durkin and Bryant (1995) suggest that the instant gratification associated with online sexual activity reinforces sexual fantasies that otherwise may be extinguished. In other words, the high rate of reinforcement associated with the sexual satisfaction of cybersex activity may be shaping preferences and behaviors that would not have been explored in real-life. This is especially concerning with the presence of pornography that is aggressive and/or demeaning towards women. Goldberg, Peterson, Rosen, and Sara (2008) report that up to 11.8 million people who engage in cybersex may have difficulty controlling associated behaviors.

Freeman-Longo (2000) identifies specific risks associated with engaging in online sexual activity, including exposure to inaccurate information about sexuality, exposure to age-inappropriate sexual material, and the potential development of sexually compulsive or addictive behavior. In considering sexually compulsive behavior, Cooper (1998) identifies five indicators, including denial, failed efforts to stop the behavior, dedicating large amounts of time to the behavior, experiencing negative impacts on one's social, occupational, and recreational functioning, and continuation of the behavior despite negative consequences. These indicators are reminiscent of any addictive behavior, but applied specifically to sexuality.

Individuals portrayed in online pornography tend to appear particularly young, allowing teenagers to identify for personally with the sexual acts being committed (Freeman-Longo, 2000). In identifying with the behaviors, adolescents are more likely to integrate them as "normal." Several "problems" associated with the development of sexualized relationships on the Internet are identified by Freeman-Longo, including that relationships are not based in reality, users may become sexually desensitized and require more extreme interactions to become aroused, and such relationships may increase the desire for "real" sex, resulting in earlier sexual experiences. Carnes (2001) describes the concept of eroticized rage, suggesting "anger and sex can be fused in such a way that it is self-perpetuating, self-destructive, and . . . independent of culture and even family" (p. 47). The sexual freedom provided within the context of online sexual activities has the potential to create such a situation.

Research has suggested that there are aspects of the Internet that encourage individuals to act differently online than offline (Delmonico & Griffin, 2008). Suler (2006) wrote extensively on the "online disinhibition effect," or those aspects of the Internet responsible for changes in individuals' behavior. Suler (2004) identifies six elements associated with these changes, including "you don't know me," "you can't see me," "see you later," "it's all in my head," "it's just a game," and "we are equals." Delmonico and Griffin (2008) identify the salient themes within these elements, including anonymity, the ability to escape, and a lack of consequences. When these six elements interact with one another and the underlying personality traits of Internet users, disinhibition can occur to varying degrees.

Young (1997) concluded individuals who suffer from depression, experience frequent disapproval, as well as significant feelings of inadequacy are at high risk for developing a cybersex addiction. Such individuals would need to be especially careful if choosing to dabble in online sexual activity. Price (2003) found that sexual offending and sexual addiction most often "stem[s] from derailed development of a healthy sexuality and sexual identity" (p. 225). Sexual issues may occur when an individual fails to meet certain developmental tasks, such as finding one's sexual identity. Within this task, it is crucial to determine one's "sexual values, sexual orientation, and sexual goals" (p. 226). He uses the term "sexually vulnerable youth" to describe those individuals who have not yet been able to develop a healthy sexual identity and, thus, are at risk of developing sexual issues. Again, these individuals would need to proceed with caution if engaging in cybersex.

Treatment Considerations

Parent information

In order for parents to adequately monitor and protect their teenagers, they must become educated themselves. Parents must be aware that even when implementing parental blocks and controls on their home computer, many adolescents are technology-savvy and able to get around such programs. Additionally, access through the public library, schools, Internet-capable cell phones and iPods provide additional means of access. Freeman-Longo (2000) suggests parents use the instances when their children are found exploring sexual material on the Internet as "teachable moments." In other words, rather than panic and punish, parents can answer questions regarding the material and discuss whether the actions being engaged in are healthy or unsafe. He puts forth a variety of suggestions for the prevention of online sexual abuse, including keeping home computers in frequently inhabited areas, such as the living room or kitchen, testing any parental control software being utilized, and offering age-appropriate online activities, such as chat rooms geared for teenagers. Furthermore, children and adolescents should be taught the "illegality, risks, and consequences of accessing and/or downloading [pornographic] materials" (p. 86). Education on healthy sexuality is crucial as well, since many teenagers may be experiencing sexual harassment and abuse. Children and teenagers should be educated as to the lack of anonymity on the Internet, since any actions made could be traced if necessary. It is also recommended to withhold Internet access as a consequence for adolescents who do not respect parents boundaries in regards to its use (2000).

Joan D. Atwood, Ph.D., LMFT, LCSW & Conchetta Gallo, Ph.D., LMFT

Clinical considerations

Cooper, Putnam, Planchon, and Boies (1999) identify warning signs that teenagers may be addicted to online sexual activity, including increased Internet use at the expense of in-person relationships, depression, seeking experiences that result in a "high," pseudointimacy, and using the Internet as an outlet for sexual energy and current sexual frustrations. Any clinicians working with adolescents should be cognizant of such characteristics, particularly if the client identifies spending a great deal of time on the Internet. Goldberg, Peterson, Rosen, and Sara (2008) propose that therapeutic assessment procedures must integrate "simple, direct questions" (p. 476) about cybersex to avoid missing the existence of a significant issue, which would result in inadequate treatment planning and intervention. They caution therapists using a one-down position to be flexible in following the lead of the client, as they may leave out crucial information regarding online sexual activities. Cooper, Scherer, Boies, and Gordon (1998) recommend gathering detailed information along four main dimensions, including action, reflection, excitement, and arousal. The assessment of these four areas covers the actual online activity that occurs, the cognitions associated with the activity, the non-arousal excitement and satisfaction with the activity, and the sexual arousal associated with the activity. Such information would be necessary for a properly informed treatment plan.

Cooper, Scherer, Boies, and Gordon (1998) advocate for outpatient treatment for the majority of online sexual addiction cases. They identify "group (psychotherapy or 12-step programs), couples, and individual psychotherapy [to be] the optimal treatment combination" (p. 162). It is easy to forget that cybersex addiction is just that—an addiction—and 12-step programs may be an appropriate support system. Goldberg, Peterson, Rosen, and Sara (2008) recommend therapists closely evaluate their own sexual beliefs and biases, in an effort to more effectively understand and treat clients with sexual issues. Price (2003) suggests that clients may benefit from "a highly focused developmental perspective and skills training in sexual behavior, dating, and relationship formation" (p. 225). He postulates that the removal of a sexually deviant or compulsive behavior will leave a void to be filled by a different addictive behavior, unless skills training is utilized to build an alternative behavior set. As many studies have suggested the development of sexual addiction stems from adolescent sexual development gone awry (Brown, 2000; Carnes, 2001; Price, 2003), it would make sense to attend to the developmental tasks not yet resolved during treatment.

Adolescents Who Use the Internet to Find Offline Sex Partners

Social networking communities, chat rooms, and dating sites on the Internet are playing an increasingly central role in the development, exploration, and expression of adolescent sexuality. Teens utilize chat rooms and instant messaging programs to discuss their concerns about sexuality and to develop creative strategies to exchange identity information with their peers. This exchange is critical to the activity of "pairing off", an important teenage expression of emerging sexuality (Subrahmanyam, Greenfield, & Brendesha, 2004). It is common for adolescents to turn to online content for sexual health information and dating advice, to begin courtships via instant messaging, and proclaim love and commitment via Facebook status changes. According to Wellman and Gulia (1998), the Internet has become primarily used as a communication tool to connect with others, and teens are at the forefront of this social media phenomenon. Developmental issues from adolescents' offline lives are reconstructed online with some important differences; the virtual world of teen chat may offer a safer environment for exploring emerging sexuality than the real world (Subrahmanyam, Greenfield, & Brendesha, 2004). Social media websites allow adolescents not only to maintain existing relationships with peers they know in real life, but also to meet new friends and broaden their social circle. The Internet offers a broad range of forums where adolescents can communicate with others about their emerging sexual identities and sexual needs, engage in cyber sex, and even find offline sex partners to further develop and express their sexuality *in vivo*.

The ease of instant communication through such mediums as chat rooms, instant messenger services, and e-mail has increased the likelihood of offline sex seeking individuals finding each other and meeting anonymously for sexual purposes (Kanuga, & Rosenfeld, 2004). This fact can be appealing to teens seeking sexual partners. Through its allure of anonymity and privacy the Internet can provide a unique environment that is quite different from that of traditional meeting places such as bars and clubs, places where adolescents are not usually granted access.

The private and anonymous nature of chat rooms also helps users shed inhibitions and disclose personal information, desire, and fantasy, in a way they would not in real life social situations. The potential for meeting a partner with common interests or desired is further enhanced by the substantial size of the online dating pool, giving adolescents of minority groups more access to individuals who share commonalities with them. For these reasons, the Internet has improved "sex-seeking efficiency in the same way that it has enhanced the efficiency of work, shopping, and leisure activities" (Retmeijer, Bull, & McFarlane, 2001).

Furthermore, adolescents are no longer home-bound by stationary computers, and are now able to access social networking websites and instant messaging programs via mobile devices, laptops, and tablet personal computers which may make parental monitoring more difficult, thus reducing adolescent inhibition to "get caught" by their parents. According to findings from an on-line survey conducted in 2000 the Internet is playing an increasing role in the sex lives of some young people. Respondents aged 18-24 who had ever met a partner through the Internet reported having found an average of nearly 10 partners that way, including 7 in the last year alone (McFarlane, Bull, & Rietmeijer, 2002). Young adults who had found a partner on the Internet were more likely be male and have a younger age at first sex than peers who did not find offline sex partners online (Holland, 2002). This indicated that young adults who look for offline sex partners online are engaging in more frequent sexual activity at a younger age. While many studies focus on the sexual health practices of adolescents who find offline sex partners online research is lacking to explain the motives the guide adolescents to seek out so many sexual partners in a sexually unsafe manner.

Homosexual and Bisexual Adolescents

The majority of research on the trend of using the internet to meet offline sex partners in adolescents has focused on men who have sex with men, with a specific focus on the safer sex practices and STI/HIV transmission of individuals falling into this demographic. Homosexual males are ten times more likely and bisexual males three times more likely than heterosexual males to have met someone online that they later met offline and had sex with (Daneback, Mansson, and Ross, 2007). In recent years there has been a significant increase in the percentage of adolescent males who have sex with males who met their first male sexual *partner* through the *Internet*. This corresponded to a decrease in the percentage of homosexual teens that met their first sexual *partner* at a gay venue, school, a public *sex* environment or telephone chat lines (Bolding, Davis, Hart, & Elford, 2007). While it seems that society has become more accepting of homosexual adolescents, these teens seem to be redirecting their partner seeking efforts from the public sphere to a more private and individualistic one found behind the computer screen.

Several studies show that seeking sex partners online appeals to homosexual and bisexual men, for whom the internet serves as an avenue for finding quick sexual encounters in the short term and allows them to practice for coming out in the long term (Daneback, Mansson, & Ross, 2007). Using the Internet to meet sexual partners is common for homosexual teens. In their study Bolding, Davis, Hart, and Elford (2007) found that half of their sample had sexual relations with a partner they met online. Of these, only half used condoms consistently, and half reported having sexual partners older than themselves. Increased age, White race/ ethnicity, history of unprotected anal intercourse, multiple anal intercourse partners, and engaging in sexual activity at a sex club or a bathhouse were also associated with meeting sexual partners through the Internet. This demonstrates that the Internet was not the only mode of meeting partners but a supplemental avenue of finding more sex partners quicker. Only history of unprotected anal intercourse was associated with risky sexual behaviors with Internet partners (Garofalo, Herrick, Mustanski, & Donenberg, 2007). It has been found that young adults who seek sex partners online are more at risk for STIs and HIV than their peer not using the Internet for this purpose (McFarlane, Bull, & Rietmeijer, 2002).

Heterosexual Adolescents

Women under the age of 25 are more likely to have met their sex partners online compared to women over 25 (McFarlane, Bull, & Rietmeijer, 2002). Unfortunately, at present, there is a lack of research on the behavior of adolescent girls who are finding offline sex partners online; the age discrepancies between adolescent girls and the partners they find (or that seek them out) on the Internet; the proportion of girls looking for casual non-committal sexual encounters versus longer term relationships; sexual health behaviors of adolescent girls who meet offline sex partners online; and most importantly research looking into the motives of adolescent girls who engage in the potentially high-risk behavior of seeking out offline sex partners online. Adolescent girls are overly sexualized, and are engaging in sexually explicit talk online behind their parent's back on a frequent basis (Atwood, 2006). Adolescent girls have become masters of constructing their perfect online selves by using photo editing software to make themselves look thinner, taller, and in some cases, older, perhaps to engage older male sex partners. However, the online interactions that lead to seeking and meeting offline sex partners are still largely unstudied.

Potential Dangers of Meeting Offline Sex Partners Online

Adolescent's relative willingness to use chat rooms and exchange identifying information with potential partners suggests that on-line venues may give them "a (potentially false) sense of security" that could increase their vulnerability to unsafe situations (Holland, 2002). Subrahmanyam, Greenfield, and Tynes (2004) note that adolescents' online interactions with strangers, while not as common now as during the early years of the Internet, may have benefits, such as relieving social anxiety, as well as costs, such as sexual predation.

Sex offenders use social media to prey on under aged victims (Briggs, Simon, & Simonsen, 2010). Due to the lack of monitoring of online content on some social media websites, like craigslist, selling sex and trafficking sex workers has become an anonymous, quick, and efficient business and a way for adolescents to get recruited and locked into the sex trade (Lavoie, Thibodeau, Gagne, & Hebert, 2010).

Young adults who seek sex on the Internet report substantially different sexual behavior patterns than young adults who do not seek sex on the Internet. Young adults with online partners reported sexual behaviors similar to older individuals who use the Internet to find sex partners; however, older individuals were more likely than young adults to have been tested for sexually transmitted diseases and HIV (McFarlane, Bull, & Rietmeijer, 2002). While adolescents are apt at socializing and meeting partners online, they neglect to take the sexual health percussions older individuals are taking to assure that their offline sexual encounters are safe. Adolescent also neglect to properly deal with repercussion of being harassed by perpetrators who look to take advantage of teens online (Ybarra, Espelage, & Mitchell, 2007).

According to Mitchell, Finkelhor, and Wolak, (2007) for females, being of Black ethnicity, having a close online relationship, engaging in sexual behavior online, and experiencing physical or sexual abuse offline were risk factors for receiving a request for a sexual picture. Incidents that involved requests for sexual pictures were more likely to occur when youth were in the presence of friends, communicating with an adult, someone they met online, who had sent a sexual picture to the youth, and who attempted or made some form of offline contact with the youth. Adolescent girls are naïve to the dangers of meeting with strangers they only met online in real life for the purpose of sex, but are easily lured in by older men or men with perceived higher status (Peter, & Valkenburg, 2010). This poses great danger to teen girls who are seeking offline sexual partners online to be sexually assaulted, kidnapped, or trafficked.

Affects on Sexual Health

Seeking sexual partners on the Internet is a complex behavior and its implications for STI/HIV infection are not fully understood (Baumgartner, Valkenburg, & Peter, 2010). Compared to not using media as a source of sexual information, learning about sex from movies and the internet was associated with an increase in beliefs that engaging in sex would lead to positive outcomes pertaining to self (eg, having sex will give me pleasure, make me feel good about myself) and with an increase in self efficacy about having sex (Bleakly, Hennessy, Fishbein, Coles, & Jordan, 2009). However, as previously noted, young homosexual males are less likely to use condoms and are at higher chance for transmission of STIs and HIV (Gray, Klien, Noyce, Sesslberg, & Cantrill, 2005). Bolding, Davis, Hart, and Elford (2007) suggest that online sexual health interventions should be developed targeting men early in their sexual careers. Atwood (2006) reports that young adolescent girls are overly sexualized online and are at risk of pregnancy and STIs due to their lack of consideration for the consequences of their online behavior.

Therapeutic and Lifecycle Implications

Developmental issues from adolescents' offline lives are reconstructed online with one major notable difference; the virtual world of teen chat may offer a safer environment for exploring emerging sexuality than the real world. Through the sexually suggestive and explicit exchange of private individual information, teens are able to pair off with partners of their choice, despite the intangible nature of social media (Subrahmanyam, Greenfield, & Brendesha, 2004). Research suggests that peers and romantic partners play an important role in adolescents' construction of their sexuality and identity (Connolly, Furman, & Konarksi, 2000). However, it is not clear how adolescents' who look for offline partners' online sexuality and identity are affected by their pattern of interaction with peers and potential partners via the Internet (Blais, Craig, Pepler, & Connolly, 2008). Teens of today are the therapy clients of tomorrow—how will lifecycle changes affect how they form relationships? How they parent? How the continued use of Internet social media will affect the quality of their existing relationships and future relationships in the long term?

Kanuga and Rosenfeld (2004) report that a diminished level of trust in intimate partners, loss of hope of sexual exclusivity with a given partner, and normalization of promiscuous lifestyles are among the changes that have been observed in young adults who have been repeatedly exposed to pornography online. In addition, there is speculation that such exposure may lead to an increasing emergence of cynical attitudes towards love and marriage. How does this relate to adolescents who use the Internet to find offline sex partners? Sex partners found online seen to be more disposable, and sought out for a hedonistic purposes rather than for the formation of a meaningful relationship.

It is important for therapists to understand the hyper sexualized and histrionic nature of adolescents who seek offline sex partners online and explore sexual scripts and meaning systems relating to this activity.

Treatment Considerations

For Parents

A study to examine the relationship between adolescent sexual risk-taking and perception of parental monitoring, frequency of parent-adolescent communication, and parenting style by Huebner and Howell (2003) was done to examine the relationship between adolescent sexual risk-taking and perception of parental monitoring, frequency of parent-adolescent communication, and parenting style. Parental monitoring, parent-adolescent communication and parenting style were all found to be important variables to consider when examining sexual risk-taking among adolescents.

It can be hard for parents to know that their child is engaging sexual activity with a partner their child met online, and adolescents are usually not open about this fact with their parents. It is thus important for parents to take preventative measures and open up dialogue with their teen about the potential dangers of engaging in sexual activity with individuals whom their children met online. It is important for parents to gain a knowledge base on social media networks, the latest online trends with teens, and their affects on the lives of adolescence so that they can maintain a conversation with their teens about what constitutes appropriate online behavior and what behavior can lead to adverse consequences. Communicating with adolescents about safer sexuality and romantic relationships can help an adolescent get better insight into themselves and start constructing their own sexual narrative in a positive and safe way. It is also important for parents to establish boundaries and clear set rules around proper and safe Internet use so that their children realize that the Internet is not an all-access-pass and that certain content is age restricted because it is not appropriate for adolescents to view.

For Adolescents

Adolescents need to be aware of the dangers of engaging in offline partner seeking behavior on social network websites (Gross, 2004). For homosexual adolescents, for whom seeking offline sex partners online is a sort of right of passage, it is important to be aware of the sexual health implications of engaging in unprotected sex with online partners. For adolescent females it is essential to understand the dangers of meeting offline sex partners online, and misrepresenting themselves in an overly sexual manner to individuals online seeking sex from adolescent females. While avoiding social media is neither desirable, nor realistic in nowadays it is essential for adolescents to be educated on how to use social media responsibly.

Conclusion

No one can deny that the impact of the Internet has truly caused many changes in how individuals socialize with each other. The Internet has made it easier for adolescents to form relationships with strangers online, as well as maintain current relationships with friends and family. The Internet has become a useful tool, especially for individuals who may have trouble making friends or forming romantic relationships during face-to-face interactions. Forming online relationships gives individuals the chance to open up to another person without worrying about their physical appearance or difficult situations. The Internet has made it easier for adolescents to find other teenagers with similar interests and form bonds with them over the web. Adolescents have even been turning to the web for cybersex. Relationships that have been formed online, cybersex has been used to replace sexual intercourse.

With the amount of changes that the Internet has caused, as family therapist it is important that we take this into account in our therapy sessions. The effects of the web can have both many benefits and disadvantages that may need to be addressed in session. It is vital that we learn more about this topic and how it affects normal adolescent development in the life cycle stages.

References

Act for Youth Center of Excellence (2010). U.S. teen demographics, health and behaviors. Retrieved November 12, 2010 from: http://www. actforyouth.net/documents/TeenDemographics.pdf.

Atwood, J.D. (2006). Mommy's little angel, daddy's little girl: do you know what your pre-teens are doing? *The American Journal of Family Therapy, 34,* 447-467.

Baumgartner, S, Valkenburg, P, & Peter, J. (2010). Assessing causality in the relationship between adolescents' risky sexual online behavior and their perceptions of this behavior. *Journal of Youth and Adolescence, 39,* 1226-1239.

Berndt, T. J. (1982). The features and effects of friendship in early adolescence. *Child Development, 53,* 1447-1460.

Bisson, M.A., & Levine, T.R. (2009). Negotiating a friends with benefits relationship. *Archives of Sexual Behavior, 38,* 66-73.

Blais, J, Craig, W, Pepler, D, & Connolly, J. (2008). Adolescents online: the importance of internet activity choices to salient relationships. *Journal of Youth and Adolescence, 37,* 522-536.

Bleakly, A, Hennessy, M, Fishbein, M, Coles, H, & Jordan, A. (2009). How sources of sexual information relate to adolescents' beliefs about sex. *American Journal of Health Behavior, 33,* 37-48.

Boies, S. C. (2002). University students' use of and reaction to online sexual information and entertainment: links to online and offline sexual behavior. *The Canadian Journal of Human Sexuality, 11*(2), 77-90.

Bolding, G, Davis, M, Hart, G, & Elford. (2007). Where young msm meet their first sexual partner: the role of the Internet. *AIDS And Behavior, 11*(4), 522-526.

Borzekowski, D. L. G., & Rickert, V. I. (2001). Adolescents, the Internet, and health: Issues of access and content. *Journal of Applied Developmental Psychology, 22*, 49-59.

Briggs, P, Simon, W, & Simonsen, S. (2010). An exploratory study of internet-initiated sexual offenses and the chat room sex offender: has the internet enabled a new typology of sex offender? *Sexual Abuse Journal of Research and Treatment* 1-20.

Brown, B.B. (1999). "You're going out with who?": Peer group influences on adolescent romantic relationships. In W. Furman, B.B. Brown & C. Feiring (Eds.), *The development of romantic relationships in adolescence,* (291-329). Cambridge, UK: Cambridge University Press.

Bryant, J.A., Sanders-Jackson, A. & Smallwood, A.M.K. (2006). Iming, text messaging, and adolescent social networks. *Journal of Computer-Mediated Communication,* 11, 577-592.

Carnes, P. J. (2001). Cybersex, courtship, and escalating arousal: Factors in addictive sexual desire. *Sexual Addiction and Compulsivity, 8*, 45-78.

Computer Industry Almanac. (2007). *PCs in-use reached nearly 1B in 2006.* Retrieved November 22, 2010, from http://www.c-i-a.com/pr0907.htm

Cooper, A. (1998). Sexually compulsive behavior. *Contemporary Sexuality, 32*, p. 1-3.

Cooper, A., Delmonico, D. L., & Burg, R. (2000). Cybersex users, abusers, and compulsives: new findings and implications. *Sexual Addiction and Compulsivity, 7*, 5-29.

Cooper, A., McLoughlin, I. P., & Campbell, K. M. (2000). Sexuality in cyberspace: Update for the 21st century. *Cyber Psychology and Behavior, 3*, 521-536.

Cooper, A., Putnam, D. E., Planchon, L. A., Boies, S. C. (1999). Online sexual compulsivity: Getting tangled in the net. *Sexual Addiction and Compulsivity, 6*, 79-104.

Cooper, A., Scherer, C. R., Boies, S. C., & Gordon, B. L. (1998). Sexuality on the internet: From sexual exploration to pathological expression. *Professional Psychology: Research and Practice, 30,* 154-164.

Daneback, K, Mansson, S, & Ross, M. (2007). Using the internet to find offline sex partners. *Cyber Psychology and Behavior, 10*(1), 100-107.

Delmonico, D. L., & Griffin, E. J. (2008). Cybersex and the e-teen: What marriage and family therapists should know. *Journal of Marital and Family Therapy, 34,* 431-444.

Facebook. (2010). Statistics. Retrieved from http://www.facebook.com/press/info.php?statistics

Freeman-Longo, R. E. (2000). Children, teens, and sex on the internet. *Sexual Addiction and Compulsivity, 7,* 75-90.

Furman, W. (2002). The emerging field of adolescent romantic relationships. *Current Directions in Psychological Science,* 11(5), 177-180.

Furman, W., & Schaffer, L. (2003). The role of romantic relationships in adolescent development. In Florsheim, P. (Ed.), *Adolescent romantic relations and sexual behavior: theory, research, and practical implications* (3-22). Mahwah, NJ: Lawrence Erlbaum Associates.

Furman, W. & Wehner, E.A. (1997). Adolescent romantic relationships: A developmental perspective. *New Directions for Child and Adolescent Development,* 78, 21-36.

Garofalo, R, Herrick, A, Mustanski, B, & Donenberg, G. (2007). Tip of the iceberg: young men who have sex with men, the internet, and hiv risk. *American Journal of Public Health, 97*(6), 1113-1117.

Giordano, P.C., Longmore, M.A. & Manning, W.D. (2006). Gender and the meanings of adolescent romantic relationships: A focus on boys. *American Sociological Review,* 71(2), 260-287.

Goldberg, P. D., Peterson, B. D., Rosen, K. H., & Sara, M. L. (2008). Cybersex: The impact of a contemporary problem on the practices of marriage and family therapists. *Journal of Marital and Family Therapy, 34,* 469-480.

Gray, N, Klein, J, Cantrill, J, & Noyce, R. (2002). Adolescent girls' use of the internet for health information: issues beyond access. *Journal of Medical Systems, 26*(6), 545-553.

Gray, N, Klien, J, Noyce, P, Sesslberg, T, & Cantrill, J. (2005). Health information seeking behavior in adolescence: the place of the internet. *Social Science & Medicine, 60,* 1467-1478.

Griffiths, M. D., Davies, M. N. O., & Chappell, D. (2004). Online computer gaming: A comparison of adolescent and adult gamers. *Journal of Adolescence, 27,* 87-96.

Gross, E.F. (2004). Adolescent internet use: what we expect, what teens report. *Applied Developmental Psychology, 25,* 633-649.

Hinduja, S., & Patchin J. W. (2008). Personal information of adolescents on the internet: a quantitative content analysis of myspace. *Journal of Adolescence, 31,* 125-146.

Holland, D. (2002). Among young adults, use of the internet to find sexual partners is rising. *Perspectives on Sexual and Reproductive Health, 34*(6), 134-146.

Huebner, A, & Howell, L. (2003). Examining the relationship between adolescent sexual risk-taking and perceptions of monitoring, communication, and parenting styles. *Journal of Adolescent Health, 33*(2), 71-78.

Hughes, M., Morrison, K., & Asada, K.J.K. (2005). What's love got to do with it? Exploring the impact of maintenance rules, love attitudes, and network support on friends with benefits relationships. *Western Journal of Communication,* 69(1), 49-66.

Kanuga, M, & Rosenfeld, W. (2004). Adolescent sexuality and the internet: the good, the bad, and the url. *Journal of Pediatric and Adolescent Gynecology, 17*, 117-124.

Lavoie, F, Thibodeau, C, Gagne, M, & Hebert, M. (2010). Buying and selling sex in Quebec adolescents: a study of risk and protective factors. *Archives of Sexual Behavior, 39*, 1147-1160.

Lee, S.J. (2009). Online communication and adolescent social ties: Who benefits more from internet use? *Journal of Computer-Mediated Communication,* 14, 509-531.

Lenhart, A., Purcell, K., Smith, A. & Zickuhr, K. (2010). Social media & mobile internet use among teens and young adults. *Pew Internet & American Life Project.* Retrieved November 12, 2010 from: http://pewinternet.org/Reports/2010/Social-Media-and-young-Adults.aspx

McFarlane, M, Bull, S, & Rietmeijer, C. (2002). Young adults on the internet: risk behaviors for sexually transmitted diseases and HIV. *Journal of adolescent health, 31*(11), 11-16

McKenna, K.Y.A., Green, A.S. & Gleason, M.E.J. (2002). Relationship formation on the internet: What's the big attraction? *Journal of Social Issues,* 58(1), 9-31.

Meier, A. & Allen, G. (2009). Romantic relationships from adolescence to young adulthood: Evidence from the national longitudinal study of adolescent health. *The Sociological Quarterly,* 50, 308-335.

Mesch, G.S. (2001). Social relationships and internet use among adolescents in Israel. *Social Science Quarterly,* 82(2), 329-339.

Milani, L., Osualdella, D. & Di Blasio, P. (2009). Quality of interpersonal relationships and problematic internet use in adolescence. *Cyber Psychology and Behavior,* 12(6), 681-684.

Mitchell, K, Finkelhor, D, & Wolak, J. (2007). Online requests for sexual pictures from youth: risk factors and incident characteristics. *Journal of Adolescent Health, 41,* 196-2003.

Model, J., Furstenberg F. F. Jr., Hershberg, T. (1976). Social change and transitions to adulthood in historical perspective. *Journal of Family History.*

Moreno, M. A., VanderStoep, A., Parks, M. R., Zimmerman, F. J., Kurth, A., & Christakis, D. A. (2009). Reducing at-risk adolescents' display of risk behavior on a social networking web site. *Archives of Pediatrics and Adolescent Medicine, 163,* 35-41.

Muuss, R. E. (1988). *Theories of Adolescence* (5th ed.). New York, NY. McGraw-Hill, Inc.

MySpace. (2010). Fact Sheet. Retrieved from http://www.myspace.com/pressroom/face-sheet/

Newman, B. M., Lohman, B. J., Newman, P. R. (2007). Peer group membership and a sense of belonging: their relationship to adolescent behavior problems. *Adolescence, 42,* 242-263.

O'Sullivan, L.F., Cheng, M.M., Harris, K.M. & Brooks-Gunn, J. (2007). I want to hold your hand: The progression of social, romantic and sexual events in adolescent relationships. *Perspectives on Sexual and Reproductive Health,* 39(2), 100-107.

Peluchette, J., & Karl, K. (2008). Social networking profiles: An examination of student attitudes regarding use and appropriateness of content. *Cyber Psychology and Behavior, 11,* 95-97.

Peter, J, & Valkenburg, P. (2010). Processes underlying the effects of adolescents' use of sexually explicit internet martial: the role of perceived realism. *Communication Research, 37*(3), 375-399.

Preto, N. G. (2005). Transformation of the family system during adolescence. In B. Carter & M. McGoldrick (Eds.), *The Expanded Family*

Life Cycle: Individual, Family, and Social Perspective (pp. 274-286). Boston, MA: Allyn & Bacon.

Price, D. (2003). A developmental perspective of treatment for sexually vulnerable youth. *Sexual Addiction and Compulsivity, 10,* 225-245.

Retmeijer, C, Bull, S, & McFarlane, M. (2001). Sex and the internet. *Journal of AIDS, 15,* 1433.

Schiano, D. J., Chen, C. P., Ginsberg, J., Gretarsdottir, U., Huddleston, M., Isaacs, E. (2002). Teen use of messaging media. *Proceedings of ACM Conference on Human Factors in Computing Systems CHI '02,* (Minneapolis, MN, 2002), New York, NY. ACM Press.

Seiffge-Krenke, I. (2003). Testing theories of romantic development from adolescence to young adulthood: Evidence of a developmental sequence. *International Journal of Behavioral Development, 27*(6), 519-531.

Simons, V.A., Aikins, J.W. & Prinstein, M.J. (2008). Romantic partner selection and socialization during early adolescence. *Child Development, 79*(6), 1676-1692.

Smahel, D, & Subrahmanyam, K. (2007). "any girls want to chat press 911": partner selection in monitored and unmonitored teen chat rooms. *Cyber Psychology & Behavior 10*(3), 346-353.

Sorensen, S. (2007). Adolescent romantic relationships. *ACT for Youth Center of Excellence,* 1-4.

Subrahmanyam, k, Greenfield, P, & Tynes, B. (2004). Constructing sexuality and identity in an online teen chat room. *Applied Developmental Psychology, 25,* 651-666.

Subrahmanyam, K. & Lin, G. (2007). Adolescents on the net: Internet use and well-being *Adolescence, 42*(168). 659-677.

Twitter. (2010). About. Retrieved from http://twitter.com/about

Wolak, J., Mitchell, K.J. & Finkelhor, D. (2002). Close online relationships in a national sample of adolescents. *Adolescence, 37*(147), 441-455.

Ybarra, M, Espelage, D, & Mitchell, K. (2007). The co-occurrence of internet harassment and unwanted sexual solicitation victimization and perpetration: associations with psychosocial indicators. *Journal of Adolescent Health, 41*, S31-S41.

CHAPTER 3

The Effects of Internet Related Pornographic Viewing on Adolescents and the Implications for Mental Health Professionals

Alexandra Volkheimer

Adolescents are among the largest group of people who use the internet and also spend the most time engaging in online activities. Some of these teens use the web to talk to friends, do research, read blogs, or post photos. However, there is another side of the internet that does not get talked about as much. Pornography and other sexually explicit material are available on the internet for anyone to use. Many of the websites say 18 or older but then just ask for a birthday that matches that age and anyone can enter. Some of these children enter on their own and some may be exposed to advertisements that just pop up on the screen. There are two sides of the debate on teens viewing sexual material on the internet. Some believe that it can actually help teens adjust and learn about sexuality in a healthy way. Others think that it can harm them by giving them a false reality and in some cases lead to addiction. There is also a difference between males and females when viewing pornographic material. The differences include frequency of viewing, reasons for viewing, and reactions to viewing. The effects of growing up with pornography at ones disposal is also up for debate. These could involve psychological, social and school related effects. The effects can also be all consuming of these children. Sometimes, an addiction to pornography can develop early and affect someone throughout his or her life. The addiction may lead to isolation, desensitization, and acting out sexually. Treatments by mental health professionals are available for these problems. Also, MHP's will be seeing more and more clients discussing issues related to online pornography. It is important that people in this field are up to date with current literature and ways in which they can help parents with adolescents. Many preventative measures can take place to ensure that exposure of pornography to younger children does not occur and that teenagers are not affected by internet pornography.

Background on Internet Usage

According to an article by Boies, Cooper, and Osborne, adolescents aged 12-24 make up the largest group of people using the internet (Variations, 2004, 209). It is not until more recent years that this change has occurred. In 1998 only 40% of homes in the United States had a "personal computer" compared with a survey done by Seagate Technology which finds that 76% of homes not contain a personal computer (Kraut, 1998, 1017). Internet use among teenagers in the United States is increasing yearly. In 2007, approximately 93 % of children from 12-17 were using the internet on a daily basis in the US. A study done by Wolak, Mitchell, an Finkelhor (2007) that 34 % of teens who are using the internet end up viewing sexual material. The focus of this research paper is on how the viewing of pornographic materials effects these teens. A term that is used in much of the literature to explain this occurrence is "Online Sexual Activity" or OSA. OSA includes "text, audio, and graphic files for any activity that involves sexuality for the purposes of recreation, entertainment, exploration, support, education, commerce, and/or seeking out sexual or romantic partners" (Boies et al.,2002, 343-344).

Many surveys have been done with adults to look at OSA. The most famous is a survey done by MSNBC looking people who had used the internet for "sexual pursuits" at least one time in their lives. The study hoped to find a different between people who used the internet for "recreation" and those who had developed a "compulsivity." This study was groundbreaking in that it was the first study of its kind with a large sample size (N=9,177) and wanted to find the implications for choices made on the internet. The study found that 8% of the sample where "compulsive users." This may not seem like a lot, but if gereranlized to the total population of internet users, 4,560,000 persons could develop problems (Gordon, 1998, 156-161).

Other studies have looked at college students and their internet usage. A study by Scherer found that out of 531 students, 15.4 % of them used the internet for OSA. "Research has yet to be conducted on the direct relationship between online sexual activities and young adult development. In an exploratory study, Boies found that 40% of his sample of university students had recently viewed sexually explicit material (SEM) online and had masturbated while viewing it" (Boies et al., 2002, 207-209. But what about adolescents who are not of college age? OSA in youths has been studied over the years, but the research seems to be somewhat scattered. A Canadian survey of 760 students studied OSA involving "dating, education, entertainment and respondents' reactions to online sexual entertainment material." The part of the study which is most important is the average age youths use the internet for sexual entertainment. The average age, according to this study, is 17.7 years old. "Seeking online educational material was positively associated with frequency of online masturbation that in turn was strongly related to online viewing of SEM and moderately to offline viewing of SEM" (Boies et al., 2002, 345-346). The youths that engage in online sexual activity may or may not be harming themselves according to varying opinions and research articles.

Varying Perspectives of Internet Usage

These "diverging views of internet sexuality" consist of a "pathological perspective" and an "adaptive perspective." The first view goes along with the medical model and focuses on addiction and compulsivity. The latter believes that OSA is "adaptive, emphasizing sexual exploration and relatedness." Many of the pioneers who studied the internet and sexual activity focused on the pathological viewpoint. According to Young (1998), "Internet addiction, as it is often called, usually implies a psychological dependence on the internet that is characterized by an increasing investment of resources in related activities, unpleasant feelings when off-line, increasing tolerance to the effect of being online, and the denial of problematic behavior." Carnes, a mental health professional that specializes in treatment of sexual addiction finds that between 3-6 % of the population could be considered sexual addicts. According to some research, being exposed to SEM on the internet over a long period of time can have negative effects on one's relationship. It may reduce the need for a more intimate connection and decrease emotions. This could have a negative impact on youth whom are still developing their sexuality (Boies, 2004, 354).

The "adaptive perspective" believes that the internet can be used as a form of sexual expression. Cooper and Sporolari (1997) came up with the term "computer mediated relation" (CMR). CMR is important to this perspective because it describes that couples may benefit from sexual material on the internet. For example: If one partner would like to explore some type of sexuality and his or her partner is not too sure, the couple could use the internet to "normalize" the urges they experience. Leiblum (1997) believes that "cybersex" can be seen as a way to communicate oneself sexually. He added to the notion of CMR that there is a "continuum from simple curiosity to obsessive involvement" (Gordon, 1998, 155). According to Davis (2001) OSA can be viewed "... as adaptive as long as it takes place for an 'expressed purpose' and in 'reasonable discomfort'—and as long as individuals maintain their ability to separate Internet from real life communication and use the medium as a tool rather than a source of identity" (Boies, 2004, 253).

Another viewpoint that goes along with the adaptive theme is the notion that OSA can be used by young people as a form of sexual education. In the article "What do people do with porn?" a study by Holand et al (1998) discusses that fact that while females tend to seek out sexual education from "dictionaries, books, magazines, and romance novels, boys used pornography . . ." Young boys used this pornographic material to learn about the female body and how to perform sexually (Attwood, 2005, 80). It is essential to note that girls and boys views on sexuality differ as does their use of the internet for pornography. The study entitled "Clustering of Internet Risk Behaviors in a Middle School Student Population" is an in-depth research project which hopes to look at risk behaviors in younger adolescents rather than the typical studies done with high school or college students. In this study 404 students were taken from a parochial school and a public school. Both of these schools were considered "middle to upper middle class" and were located in a suburban area in NE United States. The method used for this research was the "Youth Internet Safety Survey". The average age of the boys was 12.81 and for the girls it was 12.74 (Dowell, 2009, 548-549).

Variations in Males and Females

Internet use in itself is important to look at when considering the difference in female and male risk behaviors on the internet. Girls were found to have spent much more time during the week going on the Internet (M=5.30) and boys (M=4.68). The girls also had more e-mail addresses. Also, according to the girls in this study the use of the internet was significantly more important to them than it was to the boys. The internet risk behaviors also differed between the females and males. Exposure to "inappropriate websites" was reported somewhat equally between the two groups. Also a similar percentage was if they youths had "opened a link only to find an inappropriate pictures." The question if the youth "had ever sought out the topic of sex online gender was significant with 22.3 % of the boys versus 6.1 % of the girls responding yes" (Dowell, 2009, 549-550). Another difference occurred with whether or not the child had posted their picture on the internet. When this occurred (similarly for males and females) there was also a correlation to the child finding sex sites on the internet. When asked if their parents were able to prevent this, there was a significant more amount of girls (60.2%) with some sort of block on their computers compared to boys who were 49.2 % likely to have a block. Furthermore, these boys were also more likely to "override" these blocks (Dowell, 2009, 550).

An article by Mitchell, Becker-Blease and Finkelhor found differences in male and females youths use of the internet. This article focused more so on "problematic internet experiences" than it did on actual pornography viewing. However, it is still important to see what types of issues come up for adolescents. This article looked at "The Survey of Internet Mental Health Issues (SIMHI) 2003, with 35 % of participants under the age of 18 (n=521). There was a difference in male and female youths in the category of "Isolative-Avoidant Use" of the internet (66 % M and 34 % F). People with this type of use typically ". . . chose to have all their social interactions online with little or no social interaction offline; and those who spent so much time with online pursuits that they isolated themselves from family, friends, and social engagements" (Mitchell, 2005, 503). Finally, Boies (2002) finds that there are significant gender differences in whether or not the young adult was viewing SEM for "sexual entertainment" "The male-female ration for viewing X-rated material and for forwarding it were respectively 3:1 and 2:1."

Another important point to make about the difference between males and females is that some researchers believe that gender alone will determine what type of pornography or sexually explicit material the young person will encounter. According to Malmuth & Hippin (2005), when men were shown media involving a woman who was "sexually eager" they tended to have "higher levels of impersonal sexual attitudes/interest in sexual variation and of dominance/aggression motives where uniquely predictive of men's preferences (319). Men also tend to be drawn to more violent pornographic material on the internet because if they experience any type of anger and aggression toward women. Research also acknowledges that this may even change men's views on violence toward women in real life. By viewing the material they may be more likely to accept this attitude. It is a general consensus that pornographic material will have some sort of effect on the individual who views it. A quote on this position is as follows: "Pornography does have effects; it is just not yet known how widespread or powerful they really are" . . . "It may be likely that pornography's effects are important for some individuals, but not for others, and they may prime behaviors only as they interact with certain other risk factors" (Malmuth & Huppin, 2005, 324).

Effects on Adolescents

The effects of viewing pornographic material on adolescents is a topic that becomes important as more and more younger children have access to the internet. Taking this into consideration what type of problems arises for children and their development? First off, "E-teens present an even higher risk online because they often lack the physiological and emotional development necessary to use the Internet in health and safe ways consistently" (Delmonico, 2008, 435). Some of the more recent brain research on teenagers has shown that when placed in a risky situation their brains do not know how to "make good choices." There is also evidence that teens will actually "crave" more risky behaviors then the average adult. This makes sense when one considers the typical "irrational" risk behaviors of teens. Furthermore, a term called "risk attenuation" is important to note. This term describes . . . "the adolescents inability to use critical thinking and decision-making skills to discern more risky from less risky behavior" (Delmonico, 2008, 435). When risk attenuation is paired with a situation such as online sexual activity on the internet it may cause the teenager to make inappropriate decisions (Delmonico, 2008, 435).

Another important term pertaining to teens and the internet is "generalization." According to Delmonico and Griffin (2008) this refers to an adult's ability to take something they have learned and use it in a different situation. For example: An adult may find that it is inappropriate to post personal information on MySpace but it is appropriate to send it to a friend in an e-mail. A teen might not be able to generalize from an open forum such as MySpace to a private e-mail. This same idea can be applied to accessing pornography on the internet. An adolescent under the age of 18 may be aware that they have to be 18 before renting pornographic movies from a video store, but they do not mind accessing it on the internet (usually by using a fake birthday). Although they know the law, for some reason this does not generalize to internet behaviors. This will have an effect on the developmental tasks of the teenager.

The study "Variations in Internet-Related Problems of Psychosocial Functioning in Online Sexual Activities: Implications for Social and Sexual Development of Young Adults" looks at how the developmental tasks at this stage are affected. The study looked at 1,100 students who were taking a basic psychology class at a university in Canada. Students remained anonymous and filled out an online survey of 120 questions.

There were six sections: "Demographics", "Environmental Mastery", "Perceived Social Support", "Internet Related Problem Scale", "Online Sexual Activities Scale", and "Increase in sense of connection with family." The sample ended up being of 760 students, 32.4 % male and 65.4 % female. The average age was 19. The ages of 19 and 20 made up 68% of the study (Boies, 2004, 211). The results of this study are significant because they wanted to find out how OSA affected people's psychosocial functioning.

The section of the survey entitled "Internet Related Problems" refers to an assessment of . . . "seven factors: tolerance, escape from problems, reduced activities, loss of control, negative effects, withdrawals, and cravings" (Boies, 2004, 211). The results of the survey show that an online sexual activities that were focused on "seeking relationships, sexual information, and sexual entertainment" were correlated with the internet related problems. Also, "seeking sexual information and masturbating online were two activities most strongly associated with dissatisfaction with people's offline lives (i.e., low environmental mastery and low social support from friends and families) and the perception of deriving social support from contacts with online friends" (Boies, 2004, 215-216). Further findings show that students who did not use the internet for "sexual information or entertainment" had more satisfaction in their personal lives. The people who only went online for sexual activities were equally satisfied with their life off the internet.

> "Seeking either information or entertainment does not appear to be negatively associated with lower psychosocial functioning. This is likely due, as Davis suggested, to these people's ability to engage in OSA for expressed purpose and to use the internet as a tool rather than a source of identity" (Boies, 2004, 216).

Another article attempts to look at "Online Sexual Activities and Psychosocial and Sexual Development." This article is a meta-analysis on the research to date pertaining to young people's use of the internet and the effect is has on them. The negative effects of young people's experiencing of sexually explicit material online are conflicting. However, Byrne and Osland's (2000) literature review reveals that while there are varying outcomes of the effects that pornography has on young people, one aspect seems to be the same throughout. This aspect is that "erotica can have a shaping effect on behavior." A study by Weiser (2000) found that many young people credit the usage of the internet as a space to grow socially and to make a connection with other people. Despite this sense of positivity, the studies show that making connections online is not positively correlated with connections in real life. Adolescents are less likely to find social support from the internet. Also, Cooper, Scherer, et al. (1999) found that OSA may be the biggest issue, above all other types of internet usage that causes a teen to have trouble with social functioning and involvement with family. This is also true for issues in sexual development and the formation of relationships involving sexual relations.

According to Carnes (2001) there is a correlation between

"High usage of the Internet for the gratification of social and sexual needs for socio-affective regulation increases one's sense of alienation from self and others, potentially leading to relationship regression. This is particularly serious for young adults as it can significantly delay or distort the development stage that they are navigating that has to do with issues related to identity, affiliation, and intimacy" (Erikson, 1980).

The occurrence of sexual issues from this distorted development is hard to measure because it is still unclear what is considered "normal development" for this age group. A study done by Longo, Brown, and Orcutt (2002) sets out to prove that there is little research and data that when it comes to what is "healthy or not when it comes to adolescent sexuality." A way they chose to look at adolescent sexuality is that if the action is meeting "developmentally appropriate sexual needs as opposed to primarily nonsexual needs." According to this viewpoint, when a teen turns to OSA because they are feeling lonely, unimportant, having negative feelings, or emptiness then this could become unhealthy. Because teens are likely to experience these emotions as their hormones are changing and they are developing, they are at risk for developing unhealthy behaviors such as compulsivity (Boies et al.,2004, 355-356). Furthermore, according to Dr. Voth of the Karl Menninger School of Psychiatry in Topeka, Kansas sees ". . . such exposure [viewing pornography over time] as especially damaging to the young who are on the threshold of entering into an active sexual life. For them, these vital processes should be guided toward greater maturity, not retrogressively toward perversion or transient, meaningless sex" (Cline, 2002).

Some researchers have been able to link compulsivity in adulthood with early viewing of pornography for the purpose of masturbation. It has been found that these children viewed the pornography at a very young age (younger than any of the studies available) and that these they were not able to know what they were actually viewing. As far as adolescents go, there has been some research done on sexual compulsivity going on in that population. While there isn't as much information as the adult population there are some interesting findings. The fact that youths are most likely to engage in risk behaviors without understanding consequences is a big factor in them viewing sexually explicit material on a compulsive level. According to Ponton (2004) there are two reasons for the engagement in this behavior: biological or psychological. Adolescents (both male and female) who go through puppetry at a young age are susceptible to compulsivity. Youths from abusive backgrounds are also susceptible. The actual behaviors these youths are engaging in is difficult to study. While there is evidence that for the college population a viewing of pornographic material everyday for masturbation purposes may be considered problematic according to Boies (2002). Also, a combination of an anxiety disorder mixed with substance abuse can cause young people to engage in sexually compulsive behaviors (Boies et al, 2002, 257).

An article entitled "Pornography's Effects on Adults and Children" takes a different approach then a lot of other research. Part of the article focuses on actual examples taken from the authors own private practice. The article leans towards the pathological view of pornography. A specific example is as follows:

> "Example: A mother brought her pregnant 13 year old daughter to my office. The girl and her 14 year old boyfriend had discovered her father's secret cache of pornography and had imitated the sexual acts portrayed in those materials over many months. The ensuing consequences, including pregnancy, abortion and depression, were very traumatic for the whole family as well as the youngsters. The mother divorced her husband because of the complications surrounding what had happened" (Cline, 2002, 12)

Cline is suggesting that as a result of viewing pornography at a young age there are a number of effects on the young people involved and their family. She gives several other examples from her practice where she has linked pornography with negative effects. Cline also discusses why she believes some people believe that there are no effects to pornographic viewing.

Finally, the emotional effects of viewing SEM has been touched on, but only slightly in several articles. It is apparent that in a study involving "families with teenagers participating in journalism classes in four area high schools" that looked at "demographic and control variables, internet usage, personal electronic mail use, World Wide Web use, and social involvement and psychological well-being" that there is in fact a link between all of these and stress and depression in a teenagers life. All of these aspects of the study were met with statistic information that showed a small but significant correlation. In particular, "statistical interactions of internet use with age showed that increases in internet use were associated with larger increases in loneliness and larger declines in social support for teenagers than adults. Also the study shows a correlation between stress and depression with internet usage and being a teen (Kraut, 1998, 2021-1029).

Another study set out to look at "Sex on the Internet and Emotional Arousal." The sample came from 506 undergraduate students of a college in Texas. While the study does not focus on teens per se, the undergraduate students still give some insight in the types of emotions experienced with view SES on-line. Gender differences came into play during this study. "Women were less likely than men to report feeling entertained or feeling sexually aroused by viewing SES on-line. On the other hand, women were more likely than men to report feeling anger and disgust" (Goodson, McCormick, & Evans, 2000, 255). Other emotions that were frequently felt by participants included: entertainment, excitement, disgust, and worry about being caught. A final ethnic consideration of the study was that Hispanic women were two times more likely to being frequently aroused when viewing the material than Anglo women. This result is interesting because it shows that the impact of viewing pornographic material on the internet may go beyond just differences in age and gender, but also be affected by cultural and societal viewpoints on what is right and wrong (Goodson, 2000, 258).

Joan D. Atwood, Ph.D., LMFT, LCSW & Conchetta Gallo, Ph.D., LMFT

Assessment: For Mental Health Professionals

Due to the easy access of pornographic materials on the internet it is no wonder that mental health professional (marriage and family therapists in particular) have come across issues in their practice relating to young people's exposure. To be aware of a "behavior problem" a therapist may need to take into consideration the age of the child, the amount of exposure, and the effects it is having on him and his family. There are several other ways to assess for problematic behavior. According to Delmonico and Griffin (2008) "No single one of these signs is more important than another, nor is a single symptom an indicator of a serious problem; rather marriage and family therapists should gather information from a variety of perspective and look for constellations of signs and symptoms as indicators of possible problems" (437). One sign may be if the individual states he or she has been spending more time on-line in general then doing things in real life. Also, not wanting to talk about the types of activities they are engaging in on the internet may be a sign. An attempt to hide the amount of time spent on the internet as well as not wanting one's own friends to know about it could be a warning sign. This could also include deleting the "browsing history". Therapists as well as friends and family should assess for signs of depression or anxiety occurring when one is unable to access the internet. They should also be aware of times when the person seems distraught when not on the internet. Another indicator would be "taking increased risks" like viewing pornographic material in public places or losing relationships because of pornography ().

Another important assessment tool is the "Internet Sex Screening Test-Adolescent (ISST-A)." This is considered to be a "screening test" and be used alongside the other assessments done by the therapist. The screening test can also be used in interviewing the adolescent about specific internet behaviors. Some examples of questions from the test include (True or False): "I have some sexual sites in my favorites", "I spend more than 5 hours per week using my computer for sexual pursuits", "I have masturbated while on the internet" and "I have made promises to myself to stop using the internet for sexual purposes" to name a few (Delmonico and Griffin, 2008, 438).

As far as assessment goes these are just a few ideas of how a mental health professional could approach a case involving internet pornography. In addition to assessment questions and understanding how to assess the clinician should be aware of the need for more information on internet usage as it pertains to education. Also, people should be more aware of the possible effects that the internet can have on their daily lives. Although many people are not affected by the internet, there is still part of the population that does not have access to guides or educational brochures about this topic. Also, mental health professionals should be exposed to treatment options before they get put into a situation where the problem arises. Conferences and training programs should provide information to individuals. As people depend more on the internet it is only inevitable that more information will be available (Mitchell, 2005, 506).

Treatment Options

While many youths use the internet for education and exploration it is important not to automatically assume this without fully assessing the situation. Once the clinician has assessed there to be a problem it is important to implicate some sort of treatment to help the youth and his or her family. One way to begin treatment is to first try and get the behavior under control. The second part would be to attempt to discover the underlying reasons the person has developed a problem. To tackle the first the therapist may suggest to "physically manage" when the young person is using the internet. To do this the parents or guardians must be involved in the process. This management can be either "physical" or electronic". Physical management includes placing the computer in an area of the home where all individuals can view it. Also the parents may implement a schedule of when the teen is allowed on the internet. If a household has wireless, the family should only allow access to internet in areas such as the living room or kitchen where it is visible. Also, it may be useful to put pictures of family members near the computer (or on the monitor) to remind the young person not to be drawn back into a "fantasy world." Electronically, "filtering/blocking" can be used by purchasing software and downloading it onto the computer. One is able to block certain internet sites and only allow for access at certain times of the day. While this may be useful when part of an overall treatment plan, some people may rely on it too heavily for protection. There are also other types of software such as "Spector" which can be used to monitor to see amount of time spent on computer and what sites were visited. Finally, it is important to note that all of these treatment strategies depend on the adults in the household to follow through. Because teens still need parenting at this stage it is important to balance being a parent but also allowing them their freedom (Delmonico & Griffin, 2008, 339-441).

To tackle the "underlying issues" is to truly get to the heart of the problem. Monitoring usage will work in the short term, but the issue is more likely to come up again if the young person has not looked deeper into what causes the behaviors. Delmonico & Griffin (2008) suggest taking into consideration the following: "attachment issues, early traumatization, intimacy and relationship development, grief and loss issues, difficulties with physical, emotional, psychological, and sexual development" . . . "which may manifest as underdeveloped social skills, low self esteem/self-worth, isolation and withdrawl, depression/anxiety, relational conflict or difficulties, inappropriate sexual behaviors, poor coping skills, and attention deficit issues (441). The therapist should allow the teen to explore any of these areas that applies to them. Depending on the type of therapy one engages in, all of these issues could be explored in different ways.

With the average age of children viewing pornography being eleven, it is important that clinicians as well as parents be aware of what is available on the internet. Exposure at such a young age may impact every individual differently. What is important here is that we take that into consideration and do not jump to conclusions. While there isn't as much information about the effects of internet pornography on adolescents then there is say divorce, there is still enough information for people to become more aware of the impact the internet can have on children's lives . . . .

References

Attwood, Feona. (2005). What do people do with porn? Qualitative research into the consumption, use, and experience of pornography and other sexually explicit media. *Sexuality and Culture*, 9 (2), 65-86

Boies, S.C., Cooper, A., & Osborne, C.S. (2004) Variations in internet-related problems and psychosocial functioning in online sexual activities: implications for social and sexual development of young adults. *Cyber Psychology and Behavior*, 7 (2), 207-230.

Boies, S.C., Knudson, G., & Young, J. (2004). The internet, sex, and youths: implications for sexual development. *Sexual Addiction and Compulsivity*, 11, 343-363.

Cline, Victor B. (2002). Pornography's effects on adults and children.

Delmonico, D.L. & Griffin, E.J. (2008). Cybersex and the e-teen: what marriage and family therapists should know. *Journal of Marital and Family Therapy*, 34 (4), 431-444.

Dowell, E.B., Burgess, A.W., & Cavanaugh, D.J. (2009). Clustering of internet risk behaviors in a middle school student population. *Journal of School Health*, 79 (11), 547-553.

Fejes, Fred. Bent passion: heterosexual masculinity, pornography, and gay male identity. *Department of Communication*, 95-113.

Goodson, P., McCormick, D., & Evans, A. (2000). Sex on the internet: college students' emotional arousal when viewing sexually explicit materials online. *Journal of Sex Education and Therapy*, 25 (4), 252-260.

Gordon, Barry. Sexuality on the internet. *San Jose Marital and Sexuality Centre*. 154-164.

Kraut, R., Patterson, M., Lundmark, V., Mukapadhyay, T., & Scherlis, W. (1998). Internet paradox: A social technology that reduces social involvement and psychological well-being? *American Psychologist*, 53 (9), 1017-1031.

Mitchell, K.J., Becker-Blease, K.A., & Finkelhor, D. (2005). Inventory of problematic internet experiences encountered in clinical practice. *Professional Psychology: Research and Practice*, 36 (5), 498-509.

Neil, M & Huppin, M. JD. (2005). Pornography and teenagers: the importance of individual differences. *Adolescent Medicine Clinics*, 16, 285-295.

Twohig, M.P., & Crosby, J.M. (2010). Acceptance and commitment therapy as a treatment for problematic internet pornography viewing. *Behavior Therapy, 41*, 315-326.

CHAPTER 4

The Effects of
Online Dating and Mating in
Romantic Relationships

Jennifer Heffez
Ellen Miller
Dana Riger

Joan D. Atwood, Ph.D., LMFT, LCSW & Conchetta Gallo, Ph.D., LMFT

History of Online Dating

Utilizing new technologies to assist in finding a mate is nothing new. As far back as 1700, barely a decade after the invention of the modern newspaper, the first matrimonial service was created. Personal ads were placed by single men and women in hopes of finding a mate. The stigma associated with running these types of ads is not a new phenomenon either. In the 18th century being single past the age of 21 carried a deep stigma; gong to a matrimonial service was viewed as an act of desperation and rarely talked about at the time (“History of Online Dating”, n.d., para 1).

> “The courting process has taken on many different forms throughout history and across cultures. Sometimes romantic matches have been arranged, and at other times individuals have been free to choose their own match . . . One of the most significant changes in current times is the range of places individuals can potentially meet romantic partners.” (Whitty, Baker & Inman, 2007, p.1)

As newer technologies were developed over time they impacted the dating world. While newspapers would provide personal ads, telephones provided a means to respond to these ads. VHS brought us video dating and the internet brought online dating. The first release of a commercial Web Browser was in 1993. From that time on, individuals 'began to embrace the technology as a means of communication as well as a way to initiate and develop relationships' (Whitty & Carr, 2006).

One of the earliest ways for singles to meet potential mates online was through MUDs and MOOs. Similar to Dungeons and Dragons, these were role-playing games where individuals would appear as characters and communicate with each other online. Many of these games would have hundreds of these players online at once. According to Utz (2000), 77 percent of users in her study reported forming a relationship offline; 25 percent reported that the relationship was a romantic one (Whitty et al, 2007).

Other places in cyberspace that facilitated relationship development, but not originally designed for matchmaking, were chat rooms and newsgroups. Newsgroups are asynchronous discussions around particular topics ranging from a serious academic matter to a hobby or even a fetish. Parks and Floyd (1996) found in their study that almost two-thirds of their sample had developed a personal relationship offline. (Whitty et al, 2007)

Chat rooms also provided an opportunity for like-minded individuals to discuss a topic of interest but generally in a more synchronous form of communication. Many romantic relationships were able to form in this venue as well since there was ample opportunity for the participants to communicate one on one as well.

The current literature defines online dating as a purposeful form of meeting new people through specifically designed internet sites. Fiore and Donath (2004) identified three broad categories of online dating sites: Search/sort/match systems (i.e. Match.com and Yahoo.com) which allow users to search for prospective partners based on particular characteristics; Personality matching systems (i.e. eHarmony) where control over matching people is retained by the site providers and based on personality testing; Social network systems (i.e. Friendster) which encourages users to introduce people they know to the site a suggest matches between the members of the same social networks (Whitty et al 2007).

History of Internet Dating Sites

Launched in 1995, Match.com is considered one of the leaders in the online dating industry. During its first year of operation, the website attracted 60,000 members; currently, it boasts approximately 60,000 new registered users a day across six continents, 32 countries, and 18 languages joining the 15 million people who use match to find to make an online connection. Some Match.com milestones have included the launch in 2002 of 25 international local-language dating sites, the 2003 addition of advisors specially trained in dating, relationship and marriage, and the signing in 2006 of Dr. Phil, psychologist and television host, as a dating advice expert ("Online Dating Services-Match.com", 2010, para. 1).

Before e-Harmony became a matchmaking site, it was a website developed with a focus on marriage and improving relationships. In 1999, eHarmony.com contained a survey to be filled out by married couples to get an evaluation of their relationship from psychologist, Dr. Neil Clark Warren. By 2000, the site was reformatted to be an online dating site and claims to be based on"35 years of empirical and clinical research on what goes into successful relationships". Throughout its history the company has relied heavily on radio and TV advertising. Currently, the eHarmony registered user site claims to have a member count of over 5 million users and is responsible for more marriages than any other dating site. In 2004, eHarmony was granted a US patent for its unique Compatibility Matching System which is used to predict long-term compatibility between two individuals based on research conducted using more than 5,000 married people (("Online Dating Services-EHarmony.com", 2010, Para 1-3).

While some websites focus on matchmaking according to similar interests and characteristics, other focus on matching people of similar cultures, race, religion, or gender. JDate is one of the most successful religion based dating websites currently used in the United States. JDate helps match people of the Jewish descent to each other as well as those interested in dating Jewish people.

Spark Networks, the owner of JDate, runs 32 dating sites; for Greek singles, Catholics, African-Americans, Asians, Seventh-day Adventists . . . but no website is as successful as well as JDate.com. In the first quarter of 2009, JDate's national and international sites accounted for $7.6 million of the company's $12 million revenue. JDate is the oldest of the company's services, which partly explains its success. But it has also been embraced by Jewish leaders, fearful of the high rate of intermarriage; 47 percent of Jews who married from 1996 to 2001 married outside their faith, according to the most recent figures available from the National Jewish Population Survey. JDate offers group discounts to rabbis buying memberships in bulk. And while the company's home page photos mostly depict 20-somethings, the reality is that one-quarter of users are baby boomers.(Winerip, 2009,)

Characteristics of Online Daters

Approximately 37% of single American Internet users who are looking for a romantic partner have gone to a dating website. The Web has become the fourth most popular strategy in finding a date or a romantic partner, next to work or school (38%), and nightclubs, bars, cafes, or other social gatherings (13%) (Valkenburg & Peter, 2007, p. 849).

In their research, Walkenburg and Peter found that nearly half, 43 percent, of single Internet users, reported having visited a dating site to get a date or find a partner. Online daters did not share any specific income or educational level. Men reported visiting more dating sites than females but there was no significant difference in the genders when it came to posting profiles online. People around the age of 40 were the most active users. This phenomenon can be attributed to the limitations this age group may face in traditional arenas. Singles of this age are usually active in their careers and have children. Divorced people are three times more likely to use the internet to find a mate than the average internet user and display low signs of dating anxiety. This may dispute some earlier research that people turn to the internet because of some social deficit.

Presentation of Online Dater in Cyber World

Researchers on OkCupid.com, an online dating website, cataloged over 7,000 photographs analyzing how a several aspects of a person's profile picture may entice an observer to click. The participants in the survey were chosen at random from all users in big cities, with only one profile photograph, between the ages of 18 and 32. The three main categories looked at were facial attitude, photo context, and how much skin the person is revealing (Rudder, 2010).

When looking at facial attitude the most important factors studied were if the person in the picture was smiling, making a flirtatious face, or being serious. Another factor observed was if the person was staring straight ahead or turning away from camera. According to the studies, it appears that woman smile about 50% more than men do and make that flirty-face four times as often (Rudder, 2010). Although most people believe that smiling maybe more desirable in order to attract attention, female users actually received more messages when they had a profile picture that was displaying a flirtatious expression while looking directly at the camera. Overall, looking at the camera while making any facial expression proved to be more beneficial than turning away from the camera and avoiding eye contact.

Different Approaches to the Camera
by gender

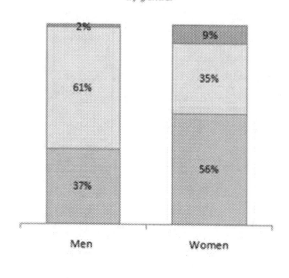

The Effect of a Woman's Facial Attitude

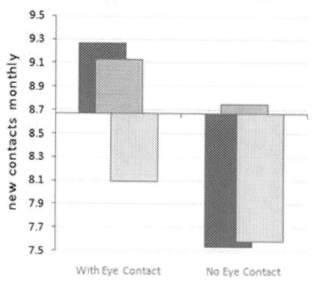

Another type of photo used frequently for profile pictures by women are is what may be known as the "MySpace shot" (Rudder, 2010). These pictures are typically taken from a high angle by the person in the photo while making a flirtatious expression on their face. People originally posted photos such as these on a popular social networking site known as "MySpace". These photos actually received more attention than photos taken on a bed, outdoors, traveling, having fun with friends, or doing something interesting. The results were so extreme that the researchers became suspicious of the findings. They attributed this high number to the fact that in most of these photos, due to the camera angle, a women's cleavage was exposed. Once they removed all pictures where the female's cleavage was exposed, and ran the numbers again, they found that the results were actually the same (Rudder, 2010).

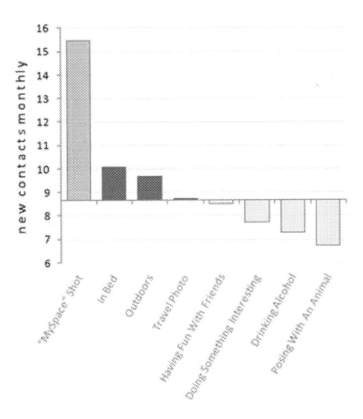

Popular Female Photo Contexts

Rudder's study later focused on women exposing their cleavage in profile pictures. Researchers discovered that although cleavage pictures did attract a lot of attention, it was the wrong kind of attention. The study was able to determine this find by counting the number of messages sent back and forth from online daters when the female had a cleavage revealing photo, and discovered that although more message were sent, many messages ended abruptly. The most meaningful messages were sent from the population of online daters who displayed a photo of them doing something interesting as their profile picture (Rudder, 2010).

According to this study, men attracted the most women when they kept a serious expression on their face while turning away from the camera. They attracted the least amount of users when their profile picture was flirty and they were turning away from the camera. A different portion of the study found that men who showed off their abdomen or muscles in their pictures actually attracted the most women. However, this only applies to men with muscles worth showing off. The statistics of this survey also demonstrate that the older you are, the less likely you are to attract women with a shirtless picture. Rudder notes that "when dating, both online and off, it is important to play up your strengths" (Rudder, 2010). If you are a man who decides not to take off your shirt, wearing casual clothing is more appealing to women than getting dressed up for a picture.

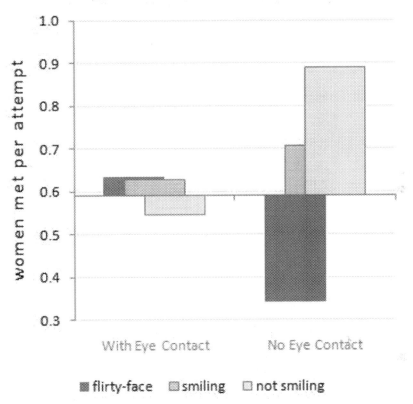

Another significant finding is that most people online would like to be able to see your face in a profile picture. However, if you are not showing your face, it is alright, as long as you are doing something really interesting, sexy, or mysterious in your photograph (Rudder, 2010). Some examples of interesting photos could be scuba diving, playing the guitar, or showing a portion of your face but leaving the rest up to the imagination.

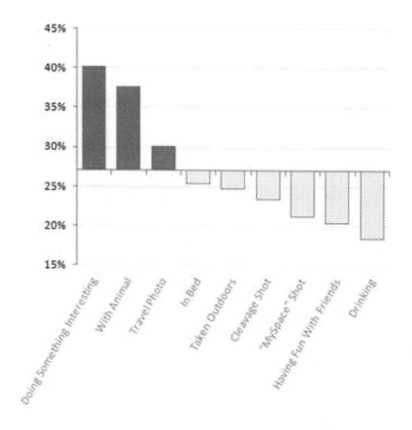

**Chance A Message Leads To
An Actual Conversation**

Overall, the type of photo that a person chooses to post on their online dating profile is extremely important. As an online dater, make sure you are aware of the type of relationship and attention you are looking to find. This information will help guide you to choosing a photo most appropriate for your profile.

Once a profile picture is chosen it is important to create a header or short phrase that accompanies your photo. The header should not be generic or boring, rather something that is funny or clever. Some examples of a generic or overused header could be, "I may be the one . . ." or "Hello . . . want to chat?" Instead, try a header such as "Willing to lie about how we met" or "Romantic men seem to be extinct, if you're extinct, contact me now!" If you are able to come up with a unique header, you are more likely to attract more attention (Tracy, n.d.). It is also important to change both your profile picture and header frequently because you may attract someone you wouldn't have with your old picture or header.

Fact vs. Fiction

Another important strategy applied to successfully meeting someone online is to be honest. Many people are hesitant to put up a recent profile picture for fear that they may have aged or gained weight since they had a good picture taken. Some people are afraid that displaying their true age will deter people from wanting to connect with them. Whatever the insecurity may be, being honest on your profile is extremely important. The truth will eventually come out once you meet in person or start a relationship and many times a relationship can end because of lying. Survey research conducted by media researcher Jeana Frost of Boston University and the Massachusetts Institute of Technology suggests that about 20 percent of online daters admit to deception. If you ask them how many *other* people are lying, however—an interviewing tactic that probably gets closer to the truth—that number jumps to 90 percent (Epstein, 2007).

There are several benefits to telling the truth online. If a person online displayed themselves as being thinner but shows up for a date and is visibly heavier, the person who they are on a date with is likely to not be happy and perhaps not want to see them again. If you put up a picture of what you actually look like and show up for a date, the person you are dating will have their expectations met or even in some cases be happily surprised in person and think that you are genuine. This allows the daters to have a great first impression and hopefully lead to a second date. "Truth is essential to dating. If you feel compelled to exaggerate so the other person will like you more, than it is not worth it. That's the beauty of dating online; the variety of choices you have to find that special person who is more to the liking of the real you" (Campbell, n.d.).

How much is too much—What to reveal when?

According to Epstein (2007), the Ten Commandments for Online Lovers:

1. Be Vague: the more information you provide, the poorer impression you create.
2. Be Enthusiastic
3. Have coffee: if you think there is some potential for a relationship, move swiftly to arrange a brief, safe, face to face encounter.
4. Don't Pay: many online sites are free like social networking sites or low cost.
5. Forget the Tests: these "scientific tests" have never been validated so it is impossible to know how to find a person's perfect match.
6. Don't get hooked: Limit online dating activities to just a few minutes a day and don't forget about the real world alternatives such as joining a club, social organization or taking a class.
7. Make contact: Don't just wait to be contacted; make the first move be initiating contact with someone you find interesting.
8. Be Honest: You want to present yourself in the best light possible but don't be dishonest—that will be a major factor in turning the right person away.
9. Involve your friends/family: look for online services that allow friends and family online to help you pick your potential mate.
10. Be Patient: In light of unrealistic claims some of these services make, online dating (as with any other relationship development) can be a slow and frustrating process.

Utilization Of Multiple Online Vehicles

These days, people are not sticking to one online vehicle as a means to find their match, but several. Some people believe that by using multiple websites they are maximizing their opportunity to meet their mate. Using multiple websites may allow people to reach different target populations and expand the selection for them to choose from. Several websites are offering their services for free, which makes it even better for people looking to use this strategy. Not only are people surfing different websites simultaneously, but also going on multiple dates in the same day. According to an article in the *New York Times*, "His 50 First Dates (or in Her Case, 3")", a young man using the online dating website, J Date, wanted to maximize his chances of meeting women but also wanted to cut costs. He stopped going on dates that involved dinner and drinks and started going on coffee house dates. He would meet a woman in a coffee house for a couple of hours and then have two more dates lined up the same day at different coffee houses. Not only did he save money, but he was able to use his time more wisely by meeting a few potential dates on the same day (Winerip 2009). Most people will know almost immediately if there is a spark or attraction to another individual, therefore, there is no need to have long drawn out expensive dates with people you are most likely not going to see again.

Similarities and Differences in Dating Online and Offline

One of the major differences online dating offers is that the control individuals have more control over their self-presentation. People can choose whether or not to post a picture, how much or how little to disclose about their marital status, occupation, or even living situation. Potential offline mates might not have any of those options especially if they share a similar social network. Similarly, since there are no shared social connections to contend with it is easier for the online counterparts to more easily terminate an encounter (Valkenburg & Peter, 2007).

While cyberspace might provide the opportunity to de-emphasize physical attributes and focus on contact on different more salient aspects of their personalities, it still plays a big role in the online dating game, according to Whitty. Similarly, this is the case in offline dating as well. With so many options, online daters may opt to bypass the less attractive profiles and make a play for the more attractive online members. Other important attributes were socio-economic status, similar interests and values. (2007)

Another difference between online and offline dating relationships is evidenced in Lawson and Leck's 2006 research: "through face-to-face relating, we have come to expect a certain pattern of flow through which a relationship develops. This pattern is reflected through the timing of conversation and self-disclosure. Often on the internet there is a pressure to disclose much in a short time to establish trust and kinship quickly."(p. 203)

Additionally, the pain of rejection is part of online dating just as it is to more traditional forms of dating. To sum it up, "the fundamental issues of trust, self-presentation, and compatibility carry over from conventional courtship into its Internet variant." (Lawson & Leck, p. 206)

Progression of Online Dating to Face to Face Interactions

A high level of personal control over the pace and nature of electronically mediated communication has been identified as a distinguishing feature of relationships initiated produces new norms of interaction. The level of perceived control available to online dating users was identified as a significant benefit of this form of dating by the majority of participants in our study (Baker, 2002).

However, through online only interactions the lack of nonverbal cues was problematic since it filtered out social cues. Partially in response to this phenomenon, in longer term online relationships, the participants used telephone conversations to supplement their online chats. This was often perceived as the next step to meeting face to face. After interacting on the phone, the next step is meeting in person. The transition from technologically mediated communication is the riskiest step in the process because it requires trust. (Lawson & Leck, 2006) and this for many people proved to be quite scary.

Adding to a potential dater's apprehension, according to Whitty's (2007) study of online daters, was the emphasis on the first date. This event was to get to know the person offline and to determine if there was, in fact, any physical chemistry. This outing was more viewed as a screening process and could even be likened to a job interview and did not have all that much to do with romance. If there was no physical attraction the budding relationship would immediately terminate.

Positive Aspects of Online Dating

The Internet provides easy and continuous accessibility to potential mates, providing almost a kid in a candy shop atmosphere. It also allows people to compensate for deficits they often encounter in offline dating world and choose only certain aspects of self to reveal online. Without having to deal with various visual or auditory clues, the users are freer to develop more meaningful interactions, increase self confidence which in turn, may lead to heightened self-disclosure such as unattractive physical attributes, disabilities, etc. (Valkenburg & Peter, 2007).

The majority of online dating sites are constructed especially to provide users with opportunities to connect with people outside their existing social network and regardless of geographic constraints. A number of respondents to Barraket & Henry-Waring's (2008) study indicated that meeting people outside of their social networks was a benefit of online dating with comments such as: "It elevates you out of your social circle, and you're sort of broadcast to a broad bunch of people, and if you're fairly open-ended in your profile, and not so descriptive about what you do or don't do, then you get the opportunity to meet lots of different people that you would never know other than that (Barraket 2008, p. 157). Additionally, it gives people new ways of exploring their sexuality. Conversely, it also gives people the ability to connect with people who share common interests, ideas, racial, familial and ethnic backgrounds with such niche sites as JDate and ChristianSingles.

The internet provides an opportunity for people to get to know each other better before they actually meet. A respondent in Lawson and Leck's 2006 study notes, "I guess I chose the Internet over meeting someone in a bar or on a blind date because to me it felt a little safer . . . On the Internet you could talk to this person for as along as you wanted to before you went ahead and met that person."(p. 204) By this sharing of information early on, important dimensions of each person's values and lifestyles and the resolution of identified conflicts may offset minor problems encountered later on in real life. Recognition of practicalities such as financial resources combined with willingness to sacrifice current comforts and nearby ties may also help people bridge large geographical distances (Baker, 2002).

Negative aspects to online dating

Barraket & Henry-Waring (2008) found that while their respondents liked the idea of personal control they also described a heightened sense of vulnerability as they became the subject of other's exercise of personal control in online interactions. For example, though an unexplained stoppage in the email exchange might be considered a norm in this setting, the participants still felt a sense of rejection and disappointment when this happened.

Online dating could be construed as making mate selection too easy and relationships too disposable. Some respondents in Barraket and Henry-Waring's study echoed these sentiments, "I wonder whether it makes everything too easy, so it can lend itself to becoming even more impermanent, relationships even more fragile. It's just too easy to meet people, too easy to cycle through people, so it kind of accelerates the disintegration of long-term relationships, that sort of thing." (p. 161)

The development of inaccurate perceptions of the people they were interacting with online. The image of a fantasy mate that has no grounding in reality, because deception is rampant online. Users can construct a more flattering appearance, inflate their incomes and job titles, misrepresent their marital status, etc. in fact, many people often cycle through a whole host on online identities.

Another negative of online dating can be the practice of cyber "stalking" which may occur since people may feel cyberspace is a safe environment to disclose very personal information in a safe environment too soon. Cyber stalking is defined as "the use of the Internet, email, or other electronic communication devices used to stalk another person (U.S. Attorney General, 1999, p.2). To combat this, there are several sites on the Internet devoted primarily to promote safe online dating practices such as cyberagnels.org. as well as other cautionary tips. It is important to remain anonymous by never giving out a real email address, home address, phone number, children's names, last name, or workplace information. Other important tips include: Doing preliminary background checks and having a first meeting in a public venue. There are also websites that conduct background checks such as CheckMate.com and WhoisHe.com/WhoisShe.com.

Future of Online Dating
Future of Online Dating and More

The future of online dating and matchmaking looks bright. Interest continues to grow and intense competition will force rapid changes in the kinds of services that are offered. In 2001, online dating was a $40 million business; by 2008 the figure was expected to break $800 million with, more than 800 businesses, large and small, vying for every dollar (Epstein 2007). "The increase in numbers of online dating sites worldwide suggests that online dating is becoming a popular choice for individuals to seek partners". Dr. James Houran, Chief Psychologist for TRUE.com, an online dating site, stated said the following about the future of online dating:

I feel the future of the industry is extremely bright for three reasons. First he rise and success of niche sites has sparked interest from new consumer markets with special needs and interests. They're arguably bringing new people into the fold. Second, new technologies are enhancing the 'tools of online dating and matchmaking' such as improved personal profiles, chat rooms and webcams, mobile communications linked to dating sites, and scientifically-validated compatibility testing. These features help overcome the past restrictions of online communication and relationship development. They simply make the process more fun and personal—it actually breathes life into the traditional personal ad. Lastly, one could argue there is a singles epidemic in society. Longer life spans, high divorce rate, and the face that people are putting off marriage till later in life mean there are more singles in society than in the past. These busy singles are short on time and opportunities, so they are looking for an efficient and cost effective way to look for and cull qualified prospects. Online dating, therefore, is actually a savvy approach to the problem (Whitty et all, p. 172).

New Tools for Dating in Cyberspace

Engage.com is a website that allows members to bring friends and family with them online to "check people out and match them up". This is the new community approach to online dating similar to what may occur on MySpace and Facebook. Though these social networking sites appeal to younger users, the "matching" that may occur as a result is not done is social isolation as is true of the larger dating sites such as eHarmony and Match.

According to Epstein (2007) the next step in online dating is already being developed—virtual dating. With the help of specially constructed software, it is reported that people who had a chance to interact with each other on in various virtual destinations went on to have more successful face to face meetings then people who only view profiles. This type of virtual interaction addresses the safety concerns some people have with meeting a total stranger in person.

Bluetooth technology developed by a company called Proxidating allows individuals to install software in their mobile phones where individuals can create a profile. Bluetooth technology allows a person to receive a phone alerts indicating when another online dater is in their immediate vicinity. This alert will be in the form of a text with an attached image included in the message. Proxidating describes on their website, "Imagine you are crossing the street when the girl/boy of your dreams passes before you, your phone buzzes and their face appears on your phone's screen" (Proxidating, 2005). Blogging might also be another way to potentially attract mates since they give a more sustained and in-depth view of a person and also allow for comments on posts (Whitty et al 2007).

Socio-Demographics

In the last decade, searching and finding romantic love via the Internet and dating websites has become an increasingly common strategy for mate selection; this search strategy emerged amid important social, demographic, and technological changes. The clientele, business returns, and presence in the media and in pop culture of internet dating have been steadily ascending. While it is still too early to analyze and assess the long term impacts of internet dating on partnership and marriage, we can identify the socio-demographics of its users. Internet dating is defined as the use of websites that provide a database of potential partners that one can browse and contact, generally for a fee. Internet dating facilitates connections that may eventually lead to face-to-face contact and in-person relationships (Sautter et al 2010).

Internet dating has been growing rapidly since its inception. In 1999, only two percent of American singles had used some form of online personals service. By 2002, twenty five percent of singles had used Internet dating services. A $1 billion industry in 2008, Internet dating is projected to grow an average of 10 percent annually through 2013 (Sautter et al 2010). The growth in Internet dating services reflects changes in technological efficiency and computer literacy, demographics of individuals searching for romantic partners and social changes reducing the stigma of online dating and making it more commonplace and acceptable.

Thus, the likelihood of using the Internet for social networking and dating will increase as individuals increasingly use the Internet more for everyday activities. The more digitized our lives become, the more normative Internet dating will become. Increasing the use of the Internet for activities formerly conducted offline will be useful in reducing the stigma of Internet dating. The more our lives become entrenched in technology, the more Internet dating will become commonplace. Beginning to use the Internet for everyday activities and chores such as paying bills, making purchases, playing games, and communicating with people may be useful for individuals struggling with the stigma of "desperation" often associated with online dating. Individuals in mid to later life, or any individual who lacks computer literacy, should be encouraged to learn how to use the computer, navigate the Internet, and utilize online services that can make their lives easier and more efficient.

Technological Efficiency and Computer Literacy

Sweeping access to the Internet, growth in technological literacy, improved real-time communication programs, and digital cameras have all contributed to a dramatic increase in the rates of online dating. As our lives become more closely intertwined with the internet for everyday activities and accessing information, it is only logical that our social lives become more intertwined with the internet as well, including our romantic lives.

Although the proliferation of computers and computer software has been widespread, it has also been unequal. According to the United States Census Bureaus' "Reported Internet Usage for Households, by Selected Householder Characteristics: 2009", the layered system of computer and Internet access is marked by racial and class-based divisions. Those who are most likely to be online have higher incomes and education, are more likely to live in a suburb or a city, and are more likely to be white (Sautter et al 2010).

The "Single" Demographic

Since 1970, the general U.S. singles population, comprised of individuals who have never been married and those who are currently divorced or widowed, has grown for both men and women. As of 2003, 48 percent of women and 45 percent of men were single compared to 40 percent and 35 percent, respectively, in 1970. This growth is due in part to steady increases in the median age at first marriage, rising from 20.8 to 25.3 years for women and 23.2 to 27.1 years for men between 1970 and 2003 (U.S. Census Bureau, 2004).

Increasing geographic mobility and relocation moves individuals away from established social networks and traditional avenues for mate selection. As individuals are increasingly traveling to college and abroad and moving to meet the job demands of a global economy, they are moving towards less conventional ways of meeting partners, and may become more reliant on intermediaries to facilitate partnership and marriage (Brym and Lenton, 2001; Furstenberg, 2003; Rosenfeld, 2007).

Social Networks, Stigma, and Diffusion

Internet dating, like other approaches that create a shortcut to finding a mate, is at odds with this traditional notion of romantic, spontaneous love (Hollander, 2004). Negative attitudes specific to Internet dating are related to safety and deception on the Internet and the type of people who use Internet dating.

Madden and Lenhart (2006) analyzed data from the Pew Internet & American Life Project and found that 55.7 percent of respondents believe that a lot of people who use online dating lie about whether they are married and 67.1 percent of respondents think that Internet dating is dangerous because it puts extremely personal and sensitive information on the Internet. Though fewer respondents indicated concerns about the quality of Internet dating users, 29 percent agreed that people who use online dating are "desperate" (Madden & Lenhart 2006).

Stigma against Internet dating may be a deterrent for some, particularly if it originates from stigmas held by close friends and family members. Just as social networks can spread stigma and discourage individuals from Internet dating, networks with enthusiastic members may do the opposite, facilitating adoption of Internet dating.

In their study of social demography, Sauter et al. (2010) conceptualize Internet dating as an initially rare and marginalized family behavior that is in transition to becoming more prevalent and socially acceptable. They believe that new behavioral norms spread as more people know someone who has engaged in new behaviors, changing attitudes toward those behaviors. This theory is applicable to the spread of Internet dating: as a changing population of singles turns to the Internet to date and tells others about their success, it may become an increasingly normative path to romantic unions.

For those individuals who are fearful of the stigma associated with Internet dating, it may be useful to simply "jump right in". The more dates people go on with people they have met online, the more normative meeting in this unconventional way will become. The likelihood of meeting individuals who have had positive experiences with Internet dating will directly increase with the number of people they encounter through Internet dating sites.

Further, the likelihood that they encounter individuals with whom they respect and admire will serve to further remove the stigma of online dating being associated with "desperate" people or individuals you may not necessarily want to group yourself with.

Education and Income

According to Sauter et al, both education and income are positively associated with higher likelihoods of Internet use. Even after controlling for socioeconomic status, black respondents are less likely than white respondents to use the Internet or email at least occasionally, reflecting racial disparities in access to technology. Younger individuals are more likely to use the Internet than older respondents, in part due to younger people being more willing to adopt newer technologies. Not only have young people been exposed to computers and computer software for a larger percentage of their lives, many have also received formal computer education, unlike their adult counterparts, thus enhancing their abilities to utilize these technologies.

The odds of being single vary significantly with age—they are very high at young ages, decline until middle-age, and then increase as people become more likely get divorced or be widowed. Although education and income are highly correlated, they have distinct effects on the probability of being single. It has been shown that individuals with higher education have a higher likelihood of being single than high school graduates, reflecting delays in marriage due to education. In contrast, higher income is associated with decreased likelihood of being single (Sauter et al 2010).

Sauter et al found that the only significant predictor of Internet dating is being divorced, perhaps because divorced respondents are still enmeshed in social networks created during their marriage and are seeking new ways to find a partner. Ultimately, patterns of Internet dating, the use of the Internet, and the likelihood of being single are influenced by age, education, income, and race. However, once Internet access and single status are controlled for, Sauter et al found that these stratifying forces no longer predict who utilizes Internet dating to search for a partner.

Personality Traits of Internet Daters

According to Mikyoung et al (2009), in their "Psychological Characteristics of Internet Dating Service Users", self-esteem, involvement in romantic relationships and sociability are major consumer characteristics that underlie the use of Internet dating services. Among sociable people, individuals with high self-esteem are more likely to use Internet dating services than are those with low self-esteem when they are highly involved in romantic relationships. The opposite pattern was revealed for sociable people, however, when they are less involved in romantic relationships. That is, individuals with low self-esteem used Internet dating services more often than did those with high self-esteem when romantic relationships were not important.

Most Internet dating sites require their users to create a user profile in great detail, including descriptive information such as physical appearance, relationship preferences, photographs, and descriptions of personalities and lifestyles. Generally, user profiles are viewed by members of the service and on certain sites even by anonymous, nonmember Internet surfers. Due to the nature of such self-promotion, some consumers may still be reluctant to use Internet dating services (Mikyoung et al 2009).

The role of self-presentation on the perceived success of Internet is extremely varied. Not much is known about the psychological characteristics that lead consumers to use Internet dating service. Due to the nature of self-promotion on most Internet dating services, the use of them among people who place great importance on romantic relationships may depend on the individual's level of self-esteem.

Generally, people with high self-esteem employ direct or approach strategies to attain their desired goals, while those with low self-esteem adopt indirect or avoidance strategies to prevent failure. This difference in the way self-esteem is regulated by different individuals is reflected in a person's self-presenting style. Differences in self-presentation among individuals with high and low self-esteem can be applied clearly to the context of Internet dating.

Mikyoung et al propose that for people with greater involvement in romantic relationships, "self-esteem is a mental resource that is needed for self-promotion on Internet dating services". Essentially, individuals with high self-esteem are better equipped to use Internet dating services. Mikyoung et al hypothesize that people with high self-esteem will be more likely than those with low self-esteem to use Internet dating services when romantic relationships are important

Further, some recent Internet surveys have reported that Internet daters tend to be more sociable people and engage in varied social activities offline as well. For example, Valkenburg and Peter (2007) found that people with low dating anxiety were more active Internet daters than those with high dating anxiety. These findings suggest that people who are sociable offline and have low levels of social anxiety are more likely to use all the means available to them to find romantic partners.

Mikyoung et al. (2009) found that people who are sociable are more likely to use Internet dating services than are those who are less sociable. This finding challenges the stereotypical profiling of Internet daters as being just lonely and socially anxious people.

Further, understanding the motivating factors behind Internet dating is critical for advertisers of these dating services as they develop their own user profiles and marketing strategies. To attract more potential users to Internet dating services, marketers need to provide a variety of tools that attract consumers.

Racial Preferences

According to a study on the "Racial Preferences in Internet Dating: A Comparison of Four Birth Cohorts" (Tsunokai et all 2009), members of the oldest generation (Individuals born in 1942 or before) were consistently less willing to date anyone outside their racial group, except when whites were the response variable. Analysis also showed that whites and Asians are unwilling to date African Americans. At the same time, African Americans are resistant to dating whites, but Asians prefer dating whites.

Joan D. Atwood, Ph.D., LMFT, LCSW & Conchetta Gallo, Ph.D., LMFT

Age Preferences

Stereotypes of older adults as withdrawn or asexual fail to recognize that romantic relationships in later life are increasingly common. According to Alterovitz & Mendelsohn (2009), in their "Partner Preferences Across the Life Span: Online Dating by Older Adults", predictions from evolutionary theory hold true even later life, when reproduction is no longer a concern. The evolutionary theory of parental investment predicts that men and women will seek different characteristics in a potential mate because of their differential investment in offspring (Trivers 1972).

The evolutionary theory suggests that men are primarily concerned with their potential mate's ability to bear offspring; therefore, they value signs of fertility, such as youth and physical attractiveness. Women, conversely, must invest heavily in childbearing and child rearing; consequently, they seek a partner who has the ability to "procure and defend resources" (Alterovitz & Mendelsohn 2009). This translates into women seeking older partners who have a high socioeconomic status.

Consistent with parental investment theory, personal ad studies of young and middle-aged samples have found that men, regardless of sexual preference and race, men seek younger partners. Throughout the life span, men more than women will provide information about status-related characteristics and that women more than men will seek status-related information.

Alterovitz & Mendelsohn (2009) found that men sought physical attractiveness and offered status-related information more than women; women were more selective than men and sought status more than men. With age, men desired women increasingly younger than themselves, whereas women desired older men until ages 75 and over, when they sought men younger than themselves.

Stereotypes of older adults as socially withdrawn or asexual fail to recognize that, with changing social norms and shifting cohort demographics, it is increasingly common for single older adults to be involved in dating and romantic relationships. Further, with the advent of psycho-sexual drugs such as Viagra and Cialis, older adults are having more active sex lives later in life. This may serve as an impetus for some older people who would not otherwise be dating, to join an Internet dating site. If a formerly impotent man, who would not otherwise be engaged in sexual activity and perhaps a relationship because of this, started dating again, the demographics of Internet daters would begin to skew a bit higher in age.

An analysis of widows and widowers ages 65 and older found that 18 months after the death of a spouse, 37 percent of men and 15 percent of women were interested in dating. Unfortunately, opportunities to develop close relationships often diminish in later life as social networks shrink because of retirement, relocation, and the death of friends and loved ones. To help combat decreased mobility and increased social isolation, older adults are increasingly turning to computers to enhance their social networks through e-mail, chat rooms, and, more recently, online dating sites with personal advertisements (Alterovitz & Mendelsohn 2009).

For women, predictions from evolutionary theory did not always hold true in later life. As predicted, women at all ages sought status-related information more often than men. The expectation that women would seek an older man held true until age 75, when they first sought a man younger than them. Consistent with evolutionary theory, women remained the choosers at all ages. Even when reproduction and protection of offspring are no longer a concern, certain mating behaviors continue across the life span.

The Future of Internet Dating

There is no disputing that the dating landscape is changing with advances in technology. With these changes, come changes in the way we define relations; the ways we define courtship, relationship statuses, fidelity, and communication. We are only just on the horizon of this new digital era, and with new mediums of communication, the way we relate to each other and engage in romantic relationships will always be evolving. The more commonplace internet dating becomes, the more socially acceptable it will become and the more people will use it.

With advances in computer education, access to the Internet and cost-efficient technologies, the Internet will no longer be as stratified based on class and race. The Internet is slowly becoming more representative of the world we live in as more and more people get online.

The roles of men and women are evolving as our needs for survival change; with that, relationships will begin to serve different functions. Advances in obstetrics and gynecology have enabled us to maneuver around the biology that was so deterministic for so long. The need to have children during certain fertile years will diminish and individuals will seek partners for different reasons.

Women are increasingly outnumbering men in numerous degree programs and professional fields. As more women join the workforce and the role of women in the home changes, women will place less importance on care status-related characteristics in men. Women are building their own statuses, making more women, and relying less on men for financial support. We are slowly but surely evolving towards a place where relationships are based less on the current evolutionary theory, an investment in offspring, and more on the level of personal compatibility, in the form of intellectual, emotional, and spiritual connections.

References

Alterovitz, S., & Mendelsohn, G. (2009). Partner Preferences Across the Life Span: Online Dating by Older Adults. Psychology & Aging, 24(2), 513-517. doi:10.1037/a0015897.

Baker, A. (2002). What makes an online relationship successful? Clues from couples who met in Cyberspace. *Cyberpsychology & Behavior,* 5(6), 363-375.

Barraket, J. & Milsom, S.(2008). Getting it on(line): Sociological perspectives on e-dating, *Journal of Sociology,* 44, 149-152.

Campbell, D. (n.d.). Internet Dating Online: How Telling the Truth Can Make Your Life Easier. In Buzzle. Retrieved November, 10, 2010, from http://www.buzzle.com/articles/internet-dating-online-how-telling-the-truth-can-make-your-life-easier.html.

Epstein, R. (March 2007). The Truth About Online Dating. In Scientific American Mind. Retrieved November 1, 2010, from http://drrobertepstein. com/downloads/Epstein-Scientific_American_Mind-The_Truth_About_Online_Dating-2-07.pdf.

History of eHarmony. Retrieved: November 10, 2010, from http://www.onlinedatingmagazine.com/history/eharmonyhistory.html.

History of Match.com. Retrieved: November 10, 2010, from http://www.onlinedatingmagazine.com/history/match-com-history.html.

History of Online Dating. Retrieved: November 10, 2010, from http://brainz.org/history-online-dating.

Lawson, H.M. & Leck, K. (2006). Dynamics of internet dating. *Computer Review,* 24(2), 198-298.

Madden, Mary, and Amanda Lenhart. 2006. Online Dating. Pew Internet & American Life Project. Available at hhttp://www.pewinternet.orgi.

Mikyoung, K., Kyoung-Nan, K., & Mira, L. (2009). Psychological Characteristics of Internet Dating Service Users: The Effect of Self-Esteem, Involvement, and Sociability on the Use of Internet Dating Services. *CyberPsychology & Behavior*, *12*(4), 445-449. doi:10.1089/cpb.2008.0296.

Rudder, C. (January 20th, 2010). The 4 Big Myths of Profile Pictures. In Okcupid. Retrieved November, 10, 2010, from http://blog.okcupid.com/index.php/the-4-big-myths-of-profile-pictures/.

Sautter, J. M., Tippett, R. M. and Morgan, S. P. (2010), The Social Demography of Internet Dating in the United States. Social Science Quarterly, 91: 554-575. doi: 10.1111/j.1540-6237.2010.00707.x

Toma, C.L.; Hancock, J.T. & Ellison, N.B.(2008). Separating fact from fiction: An examination of deceptive self-presentation in online dating profiles. *Personality & Social Psychology Bulletin*, 34(8), 1023-1036.

Tracy, J. (n.d.). Create an Online Dating Profile Header that Attracts Attention. In Online Dating Magazine. Retrieved November, 10, 2010, from http://www.onlinedatingmagazine.com/articles/profileheader.html.

Tsunokai, G., Kpowosa, A., & Adams, M. (2009). Racial Preferences in Internet Dating: A Comparison of Four Birth Cohorts. Western Journal of Black Studies, 33(1), 1-15. Retrieved from Academic Search Premier database.

Valkenburg, P.M. & Peter, P. (2007). Who visits online dating sites? Exploring some Characteristics of online daters, *CyberPsychology & Behavior,* 10(6), 849-852.

Whitty, M.T.& Baker, A.J. & Inman, J.A. (2007). *Online Matching.* New York: Palgrave Macmillan

Whitty, M.T. & Carr, A. (2006). *Cyberspace Romance.* New York: Palgrave Macmillan.

Winerip, M. (July 2, 2009). His 50 First Dates (or in Her Case, 3). In The New York Times. Retrieved November, 10, 2010, from http://www.nytimes.com/2009/07/05/fashion/05generationb.html?_r=1.

CHAPTER 5

The Internet
and Romantic Relationships

Kerri-Lynne Black
Jeralyn Buono
Michael Roche

Joan D. Atwood, Ph.D., LMFT, LCSW & Conchetta Gallo, Ph.D., LMFT

Introduction

"The potential of the internet to foster new relationships has been a topic of interest in both the academic literature and the popular press." (Hardie & Buzwell, 2006) With the advent of Facebook and popular dating websites, marriage and family therapists are forced to examine the way in which the internet impacts primary relationships. On one hand, the World Wide Web has provided a multitude of venues for people to positively foster relationships, both platonic and intimate. On the other hand, it also opens up an avenue for people who are unhappy in their relationships to seek out what they feel they are lacking. The objective of this chapter is to explore the ways in which the internet can help and hinder primary relationships.

Non-Monogamy

Finn and Malson (2008) introduce the concept of "consensual" non-monogamy. This stipulates that the sole difference between traditional monogamous relationships and the controversial non-monogamous or polyamorous relationship is that the former couple is dishonest about additional sexual or emotional encounters whereas the latter couple is open and honest about additional connections and encounters, whether emotional, sexual, brief, or long-standing. Since a large proportion of monogamous relationships will produce some form of infidelity over the course of the relationship, consensual non-monogamy should be viewed as a superior alternative.

Representations of sexuality and relationships in popular culture and living in an environment filled with sexual imagery have influenced today's society resulting in a sexually freer, more diverse society (Jackson & Scott, 2004).

"Today's adults are projected to spend a sizable proportion of their life outside of marital unions" (Sassler, 2010, p. 568). According to Sassler, individuals who enter into marriage at a younger age tend to be more sexually conservative than individuals who remain uncommitted, whether they are single, cohabitators, or serial daters. This sexual conservation most likely indicates a limited use of the internet for sexual exploration or satisfaction.

Open relationships are considered to be a relationship of the past. Couples had previously tried to maintain open relationships, believing that they would promote greater relationship fulfillment (Finn & Malson,

112

2008). Having more than one partner, individuals would be able to have various aspects of their personality complemented by more than one individual. In an attempt to appear 'normal' in society and also to create a sense of commitment, couples in open relationships had a primary partner and one or more secondary partners. The primary partner was viewed as a more permanent relationship and couples did have a level of commitment in these relationships. However, one person cannot satisfy all aspects of the partner's personality. Secondary relationships are formed to fulfill these unsatisfied areas, as long as all partners were aware that a primary relationship existed. Sometimes, individuals would interact with their secondary partner in the presence of their primary partner. In other situations, one's secondary relationship is carried out in private, as a separate dyadic entity, and discussed with the primary partner at a later time. In both situations, open relationships enabled couples to fulfill multiple desires from more than one partner.

Today, open relationships are much less common. However, it seems that many individuals still feel that one person cannot satisfy all of their needs and cannot complement every aspect of their personality. This results in the majority of individuals in relationships to stray. Emotional or sexual needs that are not being satisfied are also rarely explored in an attempt for improvement. Instead, these reasons for these voids are overlooked, and couples seek fulfillment elsewhere. Couples form relationships with other individuals to fulfill the aspect of their personality that is being ignored in the primary relationship. The internet is a useful tool in this process, providing a quick and easy way to meet new people or reconnect with old friends or ex-partners.

The internet alone may be able to satisfy unfulfilled sexual needs or desires through the ample amount of sexual imagery and pornography available at one's fingertips. Emotional needs may be fulfilled by using the internet to meet people who share similar interests or hobbies. Websites such as Myspace.com and Facebook.com allow for reconnection of past relationships, including past friendship, romantic or sexual partners. These sites are also used to create new relationships to serve similar purposes. In addition to those stated here, the internet offers other positive influences on couple and family relationships.

Joan D. Atwood, Ph.D., LMFT, LCSW & Conchetta Gallo, Ph.D., LMFT

Positive Influences of the Internet

As we move towards a generation of adults and children infused with technology, the internet has become increasingly popular in fostering new relationships. Dating websites such as Match.com and Chemistry.com have been promoted through the media for helping individuals to find their soul mate. The webcam, which is most often associated with cybersex and "naughty" behaviors, can also be used by couples who are separated by distance and wish to stay connected. Military husbands and fathers can use the webcam from time to time to speak with their wives and children while stationed outside of the state or country. E-mail messages and instant messaging are also used for this positive purpose. In these cases, utilization of the internet can maintain or even enhance couple and family relationships.

Computer-mediated communication provides a sense of comfort in seeking information on topics that may be considered taboo if discussed face-to-face. Examples of these taboo topics may include unconventional sexual practices, such as BDSM (bondage/discipline, dominance/submission, and sadism/masochism), and homosexuality, bisexuality and transgendered sexualities. The internet also alleviates a fear of rejection for individuals who are shy, and allows them more freedom and confidence in meeting compatible individuals (Sanders, 2008), or individuals who share similar attitudes about sexuality or sexual identities.

Websites and chat rooms targeting one specific demographic allow an open forum for individuals to discuss taboo topics without the fear of being judged or feelings of shame. For example, online forums specific to gay and bisexual men allow for discussions about HIV status, local men's health clinics, safe sex techniques, and information about different sexual practices (Sanders, 2008).

The internet also provides a safe space for sexual exploration among the lesbian, gay, bisexual and transgendered (LGBT) population (Bond, Hefner & Drogos, 2009). Within this population, a majority of individuals who benefit from this resource include adolescents. Adolescents often question their own sexuality and have limited sources of accurate information. Internet websites and chat rooms provide an outlet for adolescents, and many others, to obtain information about sexual practices, to meet other LGBT individuals who can provide support, and to gain a sense of community in meeting others who share common interests. Adolescents experience an online world free from judgment and stigma about homosexuality and bisexuality.

Various internet applications, such as internet pornography, allow questioning adolescents to develop and understand their same-sex feelings. Reading success stories in personal websites or blogs written by other LGBT individuals may boost confidence and encourage adolescents in the pre-coming-out stage to disclose their sexual identities to close family and friends (Bond, Hefner & Drogos, 2009). Networking with other members of the LGBT population may also decrease one's feelings of shame and embarrassment related to their sexual identities, and lead to more self-acceptance, and therefore, a higher likelihood of coming-out to one's close friends and family. Coming-out in the virtual world helps adolescents transition to coming-out in their real, physical worlds. Any feelings of fear, shame or intimidation are overcome in the virtual world, and followed by acceptance.

Some adolescents, however, may refrain from coming-out to close family and friends in a timely fashion. Often, adolescents reach a point of self actualization and acceptance of their own sexual identity long before sharing these feelings with friends and family members. Coming-out in a virtual society can sometimes result in a substitution of one's virtual community for their real one. Patterns and frequency of family communication may suffer as a result of increased online interactions, and individuals spend more time online and less time engaging in meaningful conversations with close friends and family (Kayany & Yelsma, 2000; as cited in Bond, Hefner & Drogos, 2009). However, creating and maintaining close, supportive online relationships will impact an individual's sense of self and will often eventually result in assisting the individual to reconnect with friends and family who may have been distanced in the past.

Heterosexual norms

Heterosexual norms are still evident in today's society serving as a basis for romantic relationships. Homosexual relationships are more accepted if they are long-term, monogamous, and accept family values present in heterosexual couples (Jackson & Scott, 2004). The fact that females are stereotyped to be more monogamous in nature than males may account in part for why lesbian relationships are more accepted in society than gay male relationships. Lesbian women are considered more likely to have intimate, monogamous relationships whereas gay men are viewed as more likely to engage in multiple meaningless, casual sex encounters.

Bisexual individuals face different challenges. Modern language about bisexuality concludes that bisexuality and non-monogamy are inclusive of each other (Klesse, 2005). A common misconception about this population is that an individual who identifies as bisexual must participate in relationships with both men and women concurrently. While this may be the case, it is not a requirement. Similarly, individuals in non-monogamous relationships are often misunderstood as participating in multiple, risky sexual encounters. Non-monogamous couples may have one primary partner and a large number of short-term secondary partners. However, some monogamous couples identify as being polyamorous. These individuals do not engage in casual meaningless relationships, but instead form one or two close, intimate, long-term connections.

Gay and bisexual men have the option to search for sexual partners using Men for men (M4M) websites and chat rooms. Unlike common dating websites such as Match.com and Chemistry.com, these M4M chat rooms are not intended to help men form long-term, romantic connections. The websites are commonly used for forming online friendships, obtaining information about one's neighborhood (i.e. popular venues, gay establishments), and setting up dats, but they are most often used to set up meetings for casual sex. An estimated 35-60% of men who use M4M websites and chat rooms are looking for sex alone (Sanders, 2008). The increasing availability of finding casual sex partners through the internet minimizes the appeal for committed relationships within the gay and bisexual community.

The influence of the internet in bisexual relationships or polyamorous relationships is less accessible for examination than its influence on the gay and lesbian population. Bisexuals and individuals who openly identify as non-monogamous are likely to be associated with a negative reputation and are more likely to be exposed to emotional risks in many cultural environments (Klesse, 2005).

Unlike other forms of non-monogamy that tend to focus on sexual relationships, polyamory includes relationships centered around love and intimacy. While sexual relationships may arise from these close relationships, instances of risky or meaningless sexual promiscuity are avoided (Klesse, 2006).

Monogamy and Internet Infidelity

What can we, as a society, define as monogamy? The acceptable definitions of monogamy are "the practice of marrying only once during a lifetime, the state or custom of being married to one person at a time, or the condition or practice of having a single mate during a period of time" (Merriam-Webster, 2010). As for infidelity, it is defined as, "unfaithfulness to a moral obligation or a marital unfaithfulness" (Merriam-Webster, 2010). Combined, these two definitions form a moral obligation two individuals agree upon, which is then broken by one or both of the individuals.

The moral obligation that is agreed upon is a loaded statement in and of itself. The agreement is a long standing social norm which was expected in a committed relationship. For many years an affair would be described as two adults coming together either emotionally or physically. In this day and age though, the internet has added a whole new dynamic to affairs. Online sexual affairs, or cyber-affairs, can be either romantic or sexual relationships that are first established online and remain online (Young, Griffen-Shelley, Cooper, O'Mara, & Buchanan, 2000).

This is not to say that an online relationship cannot move to the physical world, which is definitely a possibility. Henline and Lamke (2003) examined the responses from a questionnaire about internet infidelity, discussing both what it is and what the consequences are. Findings suggested that individuals were more concerned that an emotional affair, rather than a sexual one, would lead to a physical meeting. The romantic, emotional or sexual connections that develop through the use of the internet can be formed with the use of false names or identities, or with individuals playing out their ideal fantasies. These connections are less likely to advance to physical meetings. However, other online connections further develop and do result in face-to-face relationships. In-person meetings may lead to dating and committed relationships, or casual sexual encounters and extramarital affairs.

When defining an affair, one must examine what constitutes an affair. It would be best to begin with what society has been dealing with for many years, offline infidelities. Roscoe, Cavanaugh, & Kennedy (1988) focused on what individuals found to be a betrayal. Three behaviors were found; spending time exclusively with another person, having sexual intercourse with someone who was not your partner, and engaging in other sexual interactions not limited to intercourse. Taking that research a step further, Yarab, Sensibaugh, & Rice (1998) found several more behaviors which one could consider to be a betrayal. Such behaviors would include sexual fantasies, fantasies about falling in love, sexual attraction, romantic attraction, and flirting. Whitty (2003) performed similar research by asking individuals what specific behaviors would be considered an infidelity. Behaviors such as flirting, talk of sexual behaviors, and communicating emotions were considered acts of betrayal to one's partner.

When debating different forms of betrayal, one must also compare the genders. It is no secret that men and women do not see eye to eye on most matters, and infidelity is just another to add to that list. Sheppard, Nelson, & Andreoli-Mathie (1995) found that men rated infidelities as more acceptable than when women rated infidelities. Following those lines, Paul and Galloway found that women were more likely than men to end their relationship when an affair was to occur.

Although an offline affair and an online affair are behaviorally different, it can be seen that such acts that constitute an offline affair can be mirrored online. Such behaviors as flirting, sexual fantasies, sexual dialogue, secrets, emotionality, and romance all now occur online as well as in-person. Beginning to link offline attitudes to online attitudes, women rated emotional behavior as more bothersome whereas sexual behavior, although still upsetting, not as offensive (Shackelford & Buss, 1996). Roscoe, Cavanaugh, & Kennedy (1988) also saw that men were more likely to list a physical affair as a threat to their relationship, where women saw secrets and spending time with someone as more of a threat.

In 2003, about 62% of households in the U.S. had a computer, and of those about 88% of them used the computer to access the internet. Cooper, Delmonico, and Burg (2000) found that of 9,265 participants in their study, a majority of them spent 10 hours per week on the internet involved in online sexual activities. Three factors which set an online affair apart from an in-person affair is the accessibility, affordability, and anonymity provided by an online affair (Cooper, 2002).

Accessibility is the convenience one has when accessing the internet (Cooper, 2002). Wireless connections allow us to connect and disconnect from our online partners within seconds. One's online mistress may be found with one simple click. Similarly, if you are in the midst of chatting or cyber-sexing, you don't need to sweat if you unexpectedly hear keys jingling in the doorknob. You can disconnect from your online partner in one simple click and be free when your real world spouse enters the room.

It would be much more difficult to hide an affair if this same situation occurred and you had your mistress in bed next to you.

Affordability is the cost of an internet infidelity (Cooper, 2002). The courting phase of relationships is eliminated when relationships occur over the internet. Couples are not expected to buy each other gifts, take each other out to dinner or on expensive dates, and money is not needed to secure a hotel for the weekend or a motel room for the evening. Cyber-affairs are cost effective, and are limited to the price of webcams and internet connection fees. Individuals can also date, chat or engage in cybersex with more than one person in any given night without time or finances getting in the way.

Finally, the anonymity factor in cyber-affairs is the ability of the individual to assume any identity they wish while they are online (Cooper, 2002). Participants in cyber-affairs are free from worries about image or reputation. They may hide their identity by using false names or first names only, or they may acquire an entirely new identity. Either way, the thought of being anonymous often creates a sense of ease and relaxation in creating relationships. Whether moving on to disclose intimate details of one's personal life or not, the option to be anonymous is comforting to online users.

As sexualized as today's society is, a stigma still exists for some men and women who wish to explore alternative sexualities. The internet's lack of face-to-face contact allows for individuals to withhold identifying information and wear a mask of anonymity. Behind this mask, individuals are free to explore a variety of sexualities leaving fear, shame and embarrassment far behind them. Women often take advantage of this freedom to be "slightly naughty . . . (and) to try on a different sexual persona and explore unrealized aspects of their sexuality" (Leiblum, 2001, p. 395).

The anonymity factor is beneficial both to individuals with advanced social skills who enjoy close relationships (McCown, Fischer, Page & Homant, 2001), and also to shy individuals who experience difficulty forming close relationships (Sanders, 2008). The socially advanced individual is given a new, accessible forum to use create multiple close relationships, while the shy individual is provided with a buffer against rejection. A negative response received online can be easily ignored and by deleting contacts or connections, shame and embarrassment is minimized.

Champagne (2008) introduces the concept of play in the internet world. An online user only has concrete words. The user's face, body image, and intimate details can all be imagined or fantasized. Individuals who form relationships over the internet have a freedom to explore themselves in a new way, or present themselves in a different light. They have the luxury of imagination, seeing their online partner however they desire him or her to look physically. In the real world, you see people as they are. More importantly, individuals have the luxury of creativity, presenting themselves however they desire to be seen. Individuals may lie about their age, physical attributes and even gender if they prefer.

Lying in this way on online dating websites or in general online conversations is viewed as deceitful. However, the individual creating a new identity by lying in a virtual world may only be deceiving him/herself. The internet provides the possibility of being someone new, adjusting your personality, your looks, or even your gender. A user-created website named *Second Life* enables individuals to travel through a 3D world and meet individuals along the way (Champagne, 2008). The common understanding of all users entering into this world is the aspect of play. It is known that everyone you meet in this virtual world may be very different online than they are in person. A beautiful 30 year old woman may in fact be an unattractive 60 year old man. While this may also be true about the beautiful 30 year old woman you found on an online dating website, *Second Life* users understand the necessity to play. The rules of this world are extremely flexible.

Online dating websites act oppositely, forming around the belief that participants will submit only truthful information about themselves, in the interest of meeting a long-term, compatible partner. Unfortunately, this is not always the case. In the world of play on *Second Life*, it is understood that the people you meet are depictions of individual fantasies. One benefit of this type of relationship website is that the person you are interacting with does not exist in the real world, and therefore the progression of an online relationship to a physical, in-person one is highly unlikely.

With how easy it is to gain access to another person online, it's next to nothing cost, and the ability to remain as anonymous as you would like, an online affair can occur almost effortlessly. Cooper, McLoughlin, and Campbell (2000) reported that internet infidelity is on the rise, becoming more common. Greenfield (1999) reported that about 42% of internet users, who are categorized as compulsive users, stated that they engaged in an affair while online.

The internet can be a dangerous place because it opens up a whole new world where you can be anyone you want to be. Your new identity is what you make it out to be. In a survey conducted by Nielsen/NetRatings (2005), approximately 33% of the respondents admitted to lying to their internet partners. One could argue that due to this lying of who you actually are, the relationship will never move past a cyber-affair.

Even though the affair may remain a cyber-affair, it still has an effect on the relationship. When individuals engaged in online infidelity, Whittey (2005) saw that the perpetrating individual felt guilty, spent less time with their actual partner, and experienced shame and a loss of self-esteem in regards to their partner. Furthermore, if a cyber-affair was discovered, trust was lost and damages to the relationship were present just as if an offline affair was discovered.

The internet has the ability to breakdown the didactic relationship of a couple. The internet essentially begins to be triangulated into your relationship as this third person or entity. It is a medium to meet and interact with people you wouldn't normally have access to. There are many factors which can lead to a cyber-affair. Some of the factors might include poor communication, childrearing differences, conflicts, and stress (Young et al., 2000). Any marital discourse causing distance between a couple can lead to one or both partners seeking someone outside their marriage.

As suggested previously, a cyber-affair may or may not result in an actual physical meeting. Just as in a physical affair, a cyber-affair gives the individual something they are lacking in their primary relationship (Underwood and Findlay, 2004). This affair will wreak havoc on a relationship, specifically because a discussion about what is missing in the primary relationship is not taking place, and by ignoring what's missing, the couple cannot reintroduce what's needed back into the relationship.

Men and women view the cyber-affair differently. According to McCown, Fischer, Page and Homant (2001), gender differences are not present when looking at how individuals are drawn to the internet and the impact and seduction of the anonymity factor. Males and females alike embraced the anonymity provided by the internet in order to meet new people. However, "It has been suggested that men use the Internet more often than women but that women are more likely to use the net to meet men" (McCown, Fischer, Page, & Homant, 2001. p. 593).

The behavior mentioned previous, the flirting, communication about and describing sexual acts, and becoming emotionally intimate with someone via the internet, all pose a great risk to a relationship. Another behavior, which can be detrimental to some relationships, is that of engaging in pornography on the internet. Yarab and Allgeier (1998) described an important difference between sexual fantasies involving known individuals and sexual fantasies related to pornography. They explained that a sexual fantasy which is seen as attainable, such as a fantasy with a real individual, is considered to be unfaithful. Consistent fantasies about a friend or colleague in one's private time may eventually increase in the presence of this person, could lead to suggestive behavior, and could therefore be extremely threatening to the current relationship. Sexual acts involving pornography are seen as less of threat because it is far less likely for the individual to meet and begin a relationship with the porn stars involved. Since it is much more possible for a relationship to continue offline when a known or real life individual is involved, a cyber-affair is viewed as a more real threat to one's relationship than the use of internet pornography (Whitty & Gavin, 2001).

Risk Factors for the Development of Cyber Affairs

"Two individuals who have only communicated with one another through computer-mediated means are typically very comfortable disclosing personal information, seeking and providing social support for one another, and revealing intimate details about their respective lives" (Bond, Hefner & Drogos, 2009, p.45).

It has been suggested that the anonymity of online relationships is a measure of seduction that encourages rapid and easy intimacy. Things that people may not say or do in real life are more easily said or done in a virtual world where no one truly knows them. While there are several million people online every day, many manage to avoid the infidelity pitfall, so then what is it that makes a partner stray? Esther Gwinnell (2001) posits that there are several predictors that a person is at risk of developing an online relationship even though they may be in a committed relationship in the real world. Unemployment, presence of a psychiatric disorder, lack of enjoyable activities in one's life, social isolation, and marital discord resulting in one's lack of sexual desire for their spouse are just a few risk factors that have been found to be present in the examination of couple's who suffer from internet infidelity. Noteworthy is the fact that Gwinnell references a client, John, who reports feeling that there was no expectation of consequences for his actions because his extramarital relationship was only occurring in a cyber world.

Treatment Options and Implications

"Use of cybersex, can in some cases, be a symptom of a deeper relational problem, often relating to intimacy, dependency, and a feeling of abandonment" (Hertlein & Piercy, 2008, p.492). Treatment should therefore investigate what led up to the affair. During this process, it is important to address what both partners feel was missing or needed in the relationship. Often, partners develop conflict or distance in their relationship because they are afraid or unable to communicate about the things that are bothering them or that they perceive as lacking in their relationship. One of the main goals for the couple should be to establish effective communication skills and then to increase their communication with their partner.

At the onset of therapy, the primary goal of the therapist is to examine the nature of the alleged internet misuse. Cooper, McLoughlin, and Campbell (2000) suggest that relationships that develop online to the exclusion of one's primary partner may affect a number of areas in the couple relationship. These areas may range from conflict resolution, to emotional support, and to intimacy. It is therefore important to address all aspects of the relationship throughout the course of therapy.

As evidenced by the literature referenced above, the definition of internet infidelity will vary from couple to couple. Bearing this in mind, the therapist should allow the client to define what infidelity means in the context of their relationship. It is very important that as with any case, the therapist not judge the client's definitions, perceptions, or actions with regard to internet infidelity.

Much of the previous research in the realm of internet relationships addresses treatment when infidelity is the main issue. The author's of this chapter suggest expanding the use of couple and family therapies to adjust the other common symptoms present when one member of the system turns to an online relationship over the primary relationship of their partner or family. Therapists must remember that families and couples that present with problems related to internet usage should be treated within the context of the relationship, regardless of whether or not the internet usage is directly linked to infidelity.

Joan D. Atwood, Ph.D., LMFT, LCSW & Conchetta Gallo, Ph.D., LMFT

There is very little research on the techniques of treating cyber infidelity versus face to face infidelity. It is for this reason that the author's of this chapter suggest incorporating couple and sex therapy techniques that have already proven to work with face to face infidelity and other couple issues such as conflict, lack of communication, and decreased levels of intimacy, which have also been disclosed as posing problems in relationships where a partner suffers from a cyber addiction, has a cyber relationship, or has committed cyber infidelity.

Atwood and Schwartz (2002) postulate that factors involved in internet infidelity include anonymity, projection, differentiation of self, triangulation, intimacy issues, communication difficulties, mid-life crisis, and internet addiction. The author's further suggest that treatment for a cyber affair focus on five key areas: dealing with underlying issues, building communication, rebuilding marital trust, and constructing new stories (Atwood & Schwartz, 2002). At the start of therapy the couple should examine the reasons for the affair, what needs was the partner seeking to have met, were there desires that were not shared with their spouse. Communication restoration is a key part in therapy, enabling partners to discuss the affair, the possible meaning behind it, and strengthening the relationship to prevent the triangulation of a third party in the future. When it comes to rebuilding trust the initial step is for the adulterer to take responsibility for their actions. Once this has been done, the focus shifts to strengthening the couple bond. With time the trust will begin to return as partners demonstrate commitment to the relationship and prove they are deserving of each other's trust. Lastly, the therapist will encourage the couple to look to the future and write their story together. This enables the client to see that they have a say in what happens in their relationship and paves the way for what is to come.

Other approaches to treating the couple and more specifically infidelity that couples may find particularly helpful include: Gerald Weeks' systemic sex therapy and John Gottman's sound marital house.

Hertlein, Weeks, and Sendak (2009) summarize systemic sex therapy, an intersystems approach, as "a theoretically based approach that provides a comprehensive perspective in understanding the state of intimate, sexual relationships for clients and the therapist who is trying to help them resolve their sexual problems in a larger context than previously undertaken" (p.4). This model assesses for problems that may arise from biological or medical, psychological, relationship, family of origin, society, culture, history, or religion. By incorporating these items into therapy, the couple can tackle the underlying causes and risk factors associated with the development of cyber affairs. It is very important that the therapist utilizing the techniques is relaxed and nonjudgmental with clients. The therapy room should be a place where sex talk is normalized and comfort is promoted so that disclosure is not difficult for the clients.

In this model, therapy begins with a clinical interview that addresses the multiple levels of the individual and the relationship. The therapist will ask the client or couple what brought them into therapy, the impact of the reported problem on their relationship, goals for therapy, their theory for why the problem is occurring, and anything that the individual or couple has tried to resolve the problem at hand. Each partner is then asked about biological and medical factors such as physical illness, smoking, drinking, and prescription medication use. When addressing psychological factors such as levels of stress, coping, anxiety, and history of mental illness, it is also important to explore psychosexual issues. These items include the ability to fantasize, sexual self-schemas, perceptions about sex from early experiences, and family of origin (Hertlein et al, 2009).

Once the therapist has a basic understanding of the problem and its onset, duration, and impact on the couple, it is a good idea to proceed immediately with specific treatment strategies and continue deeper assessment as he or she works to alleviate distress and instill hope (Hertlein et al, 2009).

No matter the presenting problem, the systemic theory suggests an approach that utilizes multiple techniques to guide the couple through therapy. While these techniques have been specifically applied to sexual dysfunctions, the authors of this chapter believe they can be adapted to treat internet infidelity. The first is bibliotherapy and education on the problem at hand. Second, is reducing the impact of the problem on the relationship. Next is to reduce the response anxiety to the problem. Fourth, is to conduct cognitive work that will address reframing negative cognitions that maybe present not just where the problem is concerned, but permeating every aspect of the relationship. Fifth is to address fears of intimacy (Hertlein et al, 2009).

The Gottman technique is a scientifically based marital therapy, modeled on the findings of several decades of relationship research. Based on six therapeutic assumptions and several observed predictors of divorce, John Gottman works with couples to strengthen their friendship, increase positivity, and enable them to communicate and solve their own problems when possible. Each task in his therapeutic process is designed to minimize the possibility of relapse once therapy has been terminated (Gottman, 1999).

The theory that emerged from this research is known as the Sound Marital House. This theory postulates that the foundation of any marital relationship is friendship that is grounded in fondness and admiration, as well as a turning towards or away from one's partner as indicated with the emotional bank account concept. The next level up from the foundation is creating positive sentiment override which assists the couple in making successful repair attempts during times of conflict. The third level up is conflict regulation in which the couple learns to move through the gridlocked communication to fix solvable problems and soothe self and their partner. The last level of the sound marital house is creating a shared meaning system in which each spouse uncovers life dreams and goals and works towards these desired items in partnership with their significant other (Gottman, 1999).

The six assumptions of couple therapy according to Gottman (1999) are as follows. First, therapy is primarily dyadic, meaning that the therapist should only act a coach empowering the couple to use the tools learned in therapy to increase positivity and successful communication. Second, couples need to actually be in emotional states in order to learn how to cope with and change them. Research has shown that emotional learning in couple therapy is state dependent. This means that in order to learn how to navigate through and communicate emotions, the couple must experience them in session. It is therefore important that the therapist provide a safe and secure place for couples to express themselves freely. Third, the therapist should not do the soothing. It is very important for clients to learn how to self-soothe as well as soothe their partner. If the therapist played the role of soother, the exercise would not translate well to life outside of therapy when the therapist is not always around. Fourth, interventions should seem easy to do. Couples should feel that they are capable of carrying out the exercises. There is no reason for any partner to feel overwhelmed or to feel that an exercise is costly to them psychologically. Fifth, marital therapy should be primarily a positive affective experience. Gottman believes that by assisting couples to honor life dreams that are underlying their communication gridlock, friendship is strengthened resulting in a positive therapeutic experience. Lastly, Gottman assumes that he (the therapist) is not idealistic about marriage and its potential. He does not buy into high expectations or a concept of marital competence. Instead, he helps couples to reach a level of marital satisfaction and stability (Gottman, 1999). The case study below examines the ways in which each of these theories would be utilized in couple therapy.

A Case Study

John and Jane Smith have been married for eight years. They have two year old twins and they both work full time. The couple presented for therapy stating distress over the fact that they seem to be drifting further and further apart. Jane is stressed from long days at an investment banking firm that are followed by long nights with the children who still have not been able to sleep through the night. John works long hours for a high profile law firm and tends to bring a lot of work home with him. Jane complains that he spends more time in front of the computer than anywhere else. John claims that his computer usage is all work related, but Jane speculates that there is more going on. She is concerned because the couple has not had sex in a long time. Initially this was due to her discomfort with her body after childbirth, but now they both seem too tired or preoccupied to make the time for each other. John gets frustrated whenever Jane wants to talk about it and retreats to his office. Most recently John came home to find Jane trying to search his computer history which he had handily erased before she could get a look at it. During the initial session John admits to having a cyber affair with a woman living across the country. The couple conflict is further escalated when the partners don't see eye to eye on the definition of infidelity and how damaging John's extramarital relationship is to their marriage.

Analysis

Looking specifically at the above scenario with regards therapy models described above, Atwood and Schwartz (2002) might suggest investigating the underlying issues that lead John to seek out an online relationship. Assisting the couple with improving their communication will allow them to discuss what they need or feel is missing from their relationship so that they can work together to rebuild trust and strengthen their relationship.

Hertlein et al (2009) would begin therapy with a thorough clinical interview to establish what is truly going on in John and Jane's relationship.

Questions about the individuals and the couple might reveal a lack of intimacy that lead to decreased sexual interest. When questioned, John may admit to looking for a partner who is available to listen to him when Jane was not or Jane may admit to pushing John away. This demonstrates how crucial it is to conduct a comprehensive interview with couples entering treatment.

John Gottman (1999), who postulates that conflict arises when there is an underlying need not being addressed might suggest beginning therapy by assessing the degree to which the internet is impacting their relationship. At this time the therapist should seek to find out what specific activities Mr. Smith is engaging in while online. The dreams within conflict is a technique in Gottman's model that would encourage couples to investigate what underlying dreams are related to the problem or conflict they are presenting with. From here therapy can then be tailored to address both the symptoms ailing the couple such as distance in their relationship, as well as the larger issue of his internet use.

Conclusion

Internet use associated with alternative sexual practices is an ongoing topic in today's world. Continued advances in technology will continue to pave the way towards greater sexual and relational diversity, larger social networks, and a seemingly endless array of information, both accurate and exaggerated. With these technological advances, future research may benefit from investigating sexual attitudes associated with individual characteristics and demographics. An analysis of socioeconomic status and religious affiliations may offer additional insight into the development of sexual attitudes.

There is still much research to be done when considering the impact of the internet on primary relationships. Once this is established, it will then be up to marriage and sex therapists to determine the best course of action. This is where the authors of this article believe future research should be focused: on finding an empirically tested, therapeutic process for the treatment of relationships suffering from cyber usage, addiction, and infidelity.

References

Atwood, J.D. & Schwartz, L. (2002). Cyber-Sex: The new affair treatment considerations. *Journal of Couple and Relationship Therapy, 1*, 37-56.

Bond, B. J., Hefner, V. & Drogos, K. L. (2009). Information-seeking practices during the sexual development of lesbian, gay, and bisexual individuals: The influence and effects of coming out in a mediated environment. *Sexuality & Culture, 13,* 32-50.

Champagne, E. (2008). Girlfriend in a comma: Romancing on the internet. *New Media & Society, 10 (1),* 159-166.

Cooper, A. (2002). *Sex and the Internet: A guidebook for clinicians.* New York: Brunner-Routledge.

Cooper, A., Boies, S., Maheu, M., & Greenfield, D. (2000). Sexuality and the internet: The next sexual revolution. In: F. Muscarella and L. Szuchman, Editors, *The Psychological Science of Sexuality: A Research Based Approach*, Wiley Press, NewYork (2000), pp. 519-545.

Cooper, A., McLoughlin, I. P., & Campbell, K. M. (2000). Sexuality in cyberspace: Update for the 21st century. *CyberPsychology & Behavior,* 3(4), 521-536.

Finn, M. & Malson, H. (2008). Speaking of home truth: (Re)productions of dyadic-containment in non-monogamous relationships. *British Journal of Social Psychology, 47,* 519-533.

Gottman, J.M. (1999). The marriage clinic: A scientifically based marital therapy. New York: W.W. Norton & Company.

Greenfield, D. N. (1999). *Virtual addiction: Sometimes new technology can create new problems.* Retrieved November 16, 2010, from http://www.virtual-addiction.com/pdf/nature_internet_addiction.pdf

Gwinnell, E. (2001). Risk factors for the development of internet adultery. *Journal of Sex Education and Therapy, 26*(1), 45-50.

Hardie, E. & Buzwell, S. (2006). Finding love online: The nature and frequency of Australian adults' internet relationships. *Australian journal of emerging technologies and society, 4*(1), 1-14.

Hertlein, K.M. & Piercy, F.P. (2008). Therapists' assessment and treatment of internet Infidelity Cases. *Journal of marital and family therapy, 34*(4), 481-497.

Hertlein, K.M., Weeks, G.R., & Sendak, S.K. (2009). A clinician's guide to systemic sex therapy. New York: Taylor & Francis Group, LLC.

Infidelity. 2010. In *Merriam-Webster Online Dictionary*. Retrieved Novembe 15, 2010, from http://www.merriam-webster.com/dictionary/infidelity?show=0&t=1289870839

Jackson, S. & Scott, S. (2004). Sexual antinomies in late modernity. *Sexualities, 7 (2),* 233-248.

Klesse, C. (2005). Bisexual women, non-monogamy and differentialist anti-promiscuity discourses. *Sexualities, 8 (4),* 445-464.

Klesse, C. (2006). Polyamory and its 'others': Contesting the terms of non-monogamy. *Sexualities, 9 (5),* 565-583.

Leiblum, S. R. (2001). Review: Women, sex and the internet. *Sexual and Relationship Therapy, 16 (4),* 389-405.

McCown, J. A., Fischer, D., Page, R., & Homant, M. (2001). Internet relationships: People who meet people. *CyberPsychology & Behavior, 4 (5),* 593-596.

Monogamy. 2010. In *Merriam-Webster Online Dictionary*. Retrieved Novembe 15, 2010, from http://www.merriam-webster.com/dictionary/monogamy

Nielsen/NetRatings. (2005). *The Nielsen/NetRatings online dating survey.* Retrieved November 16,2010, from http://www.nielsen-netratings.com/

Paul, L., & Galloway, J. (1994). Sexual jealousy: gender differences in response to partner and rival. *Aggressive Behavior,* 20, 203-211.

Roscoe, B., Cavanaugh, L.E., & Kennedy, D.R. (1988). Dating infidelity: behaviors reasons, and consequences. *Adolescence* 23:35-43.

Sanders, T. C. (2008). M4M chat rooms: Individual socialization and sexual autonomy. *Culture, Health & Sexualtiy,* 10 (3), 263-276.

Sassler, S. (2010). Partnering across the life course: Sex, Relationships, and mate selection. *Journal of Marriage and Family Therapy,* 72, 557-575.

Shackelford, T.K., & Buss D.M. (1996). Betrayal in mateships, friendships, and coalitions. *Personality and Social Psychology,* 22, 1151-1164.

Sheppard, V.J., Nelson, E.S., & Andreoli-Mathie, V. (1995). Dating relationships and infidelity: Attitudes and behaviors. *Journal of Sex and Marital Therapy,* 21, 202-212.

Underwood, H., & Findlay, B. (2004). Internet relationships and their impact on primary relationships. *Behaviour Change, 21*(4), 127-140.

Whitty, M. T. (2005). The realness of cybercheating: Men's and women's representations of unfaithful Internet relationships. *Social Science Computer Review, 23*(1), 57-67.

Whitty, M.,&Gavin, J. (2001). Age/sex/location: Uncovering the social cues in the development of online relationships. *CyberPsychology and Behavior, 4*(5), 623-630.

Yarab, P.E., Sensibaugh, C.C., & Rice Allgeier, E. (1998). More than just sex: Gender differences in the incidence of self-defined unfaithful behavior in heterosexual dating relationships. *Journal of Psychology & Human Sexuality,* 10, 45-57.

Young, K. S., Griffin-Shelley, E., Cooper, A., O'Mara, J., & Buchanan, J. (2000). Online infidelity: A new dimension in couple relationships with implications for evaluation and treatment. *Sexual Addiction & Compulsivity, 7*, 59-74.

CHAPTER 6

Cyber-Affairs: "What's the Big Deal?"

Therapeutic Considerations

By

Joan D. Atwood, Ph.D.[*]

[*] Joan D. Atwood Ph.D. is a Professor of Marriage and Family Therapy and is the President and Clinical Director of Marriage and Family Therapists of New York

Joan D. Atwood, Ph.D., LMFT, LCSW & Conchetta Gallo, Ph.D., LMFT

Abstract

It can be estimated that 50-60% of married men and 45-55% of married women engage in extramarital sex at some time or another during their marriage and almost half come to therapy because of it. On-line infidelity accounts for a growing trend in reasons given for divorce according to the President of the American Academy of Matrimonial Lawyers and it is believed that it has been greatly underestimated. Because of the unfamiliarity and newness of this type of infidelity, mental health professionals are often unfamiliar with the dynamics associated with the concept of cyber-affairs and "virtual cheating." Many in fact do not consider the behavior as infidelity.

It is the purpose of this paper to explore this phenomenon, the cyber-affair, and examine the factors influencing it, the unique problems associated with this type of affair, along with a discussion of the therapeutic considerations.

Definition of Internet Infidelity

In 2000, the New York Times reported that about one in four regular Internet users, or 21 million Americans, visited one of the more than 60,000 sex sites on the web at least once a month (New York Times, October 23, 2000). It is not unreasonable to suspect that many of these individuals were in a couple relationship and that many of them exgaged in chat-room activities (Schneider, 2001). It is difficult to define the cyber-affair just as it is difficult to define infidelity in the non-cyber world (Atwood et al). Internet infidelity in this paper is described as an infidelity that consists of taking energy of any sort (thoughts, feelings and behaviors) outside of the committed relationship in such a way that it damages interactions between the couple and negatively impacts the intimacy in the relationship. This is based on the assumption that anything that is deliberately hidden from a partner can create an emotional distance that could present a serious problem in the relationship (Shaw, 1997).

Lusterman (1998) defines infidelity as the breach of trust. He states that one significant element of the mutual trust in a marriage is the unspoken vow that the couple will remain sexually exclusive. Another is that there is a certain level of emotional intimacy that is reserved for the couple, not to be shared with others. Pittman and Pittman-Wagers (1995) agree and state that secrecy is a primary factor in the definition of infidelity. Infidelity then depends a great deal on the couple's understanding of the contract they have with one another and additionally when they define that contract as being threatened.

Internet infidelity is different from other traditional infidelities in that it appears to be anonymous and relatively safe, as it can be pursued in the privacy of one's own home or office. One's identity can be completely obscured or misrepresented. It can also be pursued any time, day or night with not much effort, seemingly not interfering with the individual's day to day living. Thus, some of the "signs" that a person is engaging in Internet infidelity would be: going to the computer in the middle of the night when everyone is sleeping, an escalation of time spent on the computer, demand for privacy, lying about computer activities, lack of interest in communicating with spouse, sexually or otherwise, unavailability to children because of computer activities, sudden additional time spent at work, etc.

When two people interact over the Internet, the conversation generally offers unconditional support and comfort. This electronic bond can offer the fantasy of the excitement, romance and passion that may be missing in the current relationship. Instead of dealing with how to confront the issues of conflict in the marriage, the individuals use the cyber-relationship as an easy escape from the "real" issues. The Internet infidelity can become a means of coping with unresolved issues or unexpressed anger toward a partner as an outside person electronically offers understanding and comfort for hurt feelings (Young, O'Mara, & Buchanan, 1999).

Types of Internet Infidelity

Like traditional infidelity, there are various types of cyber-relationships. Cooper, Putnam, Planchone and Bois (1999) divided cyber-sex users into three categories: recreational users, "at risk" users, and sexually compulsive users. Recreational users accessed on-line sexual connections out of curiosity; sexually compulsive users spent at least 11 hours per week on-line engaged in cyber-sex activities; at risk persons were persons who had no prior history of sexual on-line activity yet when afforded the opportunity and the time spend substantial time and energy on line engaged in cyber-sex activities. Internet infidelity is based primarily on the extent of the interaction and the emotional commitment of the Surfer (the spouse committing the Internet infidelity) gives to the Internet and his or her cyber-friends. The continuum of involvement extends from simple curiosity, which is characteristic of most adults, to obsessive involvement, more characteristic of sex or relationship addicts.

When the subtle power, instant gratification and almost universal wish to be found interesting, attractive, and desirable come together, the unsuspecting user may find him or herself in a rapidly accelerating relationship with a momentum and life of its own.

The Cyber-Flirt (Chatting in Cyber-space)

The Cyber-Flirt is a surfer who logs on to the Internet to chat with Cyber-friends. The interactions can be on-line chats taking place in chat rooms, newsgroups, or IM's (instant messages). This type of interaction can become a problem for the couple when the Surfer goes on to the Internet to chat with the cyber-friends instead of spending time with his or her spouse or if the Cyber-Flirt begins telling marital problems to the cyber-friend.

The Cyber-Flirt is similar to Pittman & Pittman-Wagers's (1995) "Accidental Infidelity." These affairs are not expected, familiar or predictable. Their participants did not seek each other out. They happened unexpectedly, by chance, even carelessly, with no real consideration of the consequence" (Pittman & Pittman-Wagers, 1995, p. 301).

The danger is that the "harmless" on-line flirting interactions appear to become far more intense more quickly. Direct and explicit comments regarding sexual behavior can create a hyper stimulating effect and easily cross the line between innocent flirting and overt sexual interaction.

The progression between flirting and sexuality can become accelerated and the typical warning signals that alert one to infidelity can go unrecognized in cyber-space. Flirting suggests a limit or boundary embedded within. In cyber-space these usual markers are absent. The nonverbal signs of discomfort, smiles, and/or laughter are not available. Instead, an amorphous, uncharted, psychosocial vacuum exists which offers no resistance to the imaginative sexual impulses. In these cases, flirting can rapidly escalate to overt sexual interaction with little awareness on the parts of either member of the couple" (Greenfield & Cooper, 1994, p. 1) and can thus threaten the couple's relationship.

Cyber-Sex

In this case, cyber-sex is defined when the surfer goes on the Internet to achieve sexual satisfaction, rather than gaining sexual satisfaction from his or her partner. The continuum of involvement extends from having casual cyber-sex with users in sex chat rooms and sexual web sites to intimate sexual relations with one particular user. In addition, Schnarch (1997) believes that sex on the Internet is more like having an affair than having an ongoing relationship. "People often do things with less important partners, or when they are anonymous, that they cannot self-validate with a familiar significant spouse" (p. 18). Some seek outlets for their eroticism on-line in ways that they cannot validate and maintain in their primary relationship. They seek gratification thinking they are not jeopardizing their relationship.

Joan D. Atwood, Ph.D., LMFT, LCSW & Conchetta Gallo, Ph.D., LMFT

The Cyber-Affair

The Cyber-Affair is defined as when one partner shares an emotional connection with one participating cyber-friend on the Internet. They use a great deal of their time thinking about each other and writing to each other. In this case, the cyber-couple is deeply involved. They may even take the relationship a step further and talk on the phone. This may or may not involve cyber-sex. Often it does. If the couple live relatively close to each other, they may decide to meet. Even if they are geographically far apart, they may decide to meet. As Lusterman (1998) points out, an affair takes place over time. It may be very emotionally intense, and it may or may not involve sexual intercourse. "In a committed relationship if there is a secret sexual and/or romantic involvement outside of the relationship, it's experienced as an infidelity" (Lusterman, 1998, p. 18). Pittman and Pittman-Wagers (1995) state that romantic experience tends to occur at point of transition in people's lives, and it can serve the purpose of distracting them from having to change and adapt to new circumstances or a new stage of development. "Romance is an escape from too much reality; it is running away into fantasyland. It resembles a manic episode" (Pittman & Pittman-Wager, 1995, p. 304).

Factors Influencing Internet Infidelity

Listed below are eight potential factors that are related or set the stage for Internet infidelity.

Cyber-Infidelity is Anonymous

The anonymity associated with electronic communication allows the surfer to feel more open and free in talking with other users. The privacy of the cyber-space allows the surfer to share intimate feelings often reserved for a significant other. This may open the door to potential cyber-affair. Anonymity allows the surfer a greater sense of perceived control over the content, tone, and nature of the on-line experience. The person who is shy, obese, bald, etc. is transformed into Prince Charming in this electronic anonymous world. The surfer can create his or her own social conventions and define his or her own ground rules for social and sexual interaction. It allows the surfer to secretly engage in erotic chats with little or no fear of being caught by his or her spouse (Cooper, 2002).

The Cyber-Surfer Projects an Ideal Mate

When reading a typed message, there is a strong tendency to project—sometimes unconsciously—one's own expectations, wishes, anxieties and/or fears into what the person wrote. There is a high possibility of the surfer distorting the person's intended meaning. It is possible that perhaps all computer transference involves a blending of the user's mind with the "cyber-space" created by the machine. Cyber-space is indeed a psychological space, an extension of the user's intrapsychic world. Computers create a transitional space—an intermediate zone between self and other—where identifications, partial identifications, internalization and introjects interact with each other. This can explain how users react to other people they encounter in cyber-space. Communicating only by typed text in e-mail, chat rooms and newsgroups results in a highly ambiguous environment. The other person is not seen or heard—they are a shadowy figure, a screen or backdrop onto which any variety of transference reactions can be launched (Suler, 1998).

Cyber-Infidelity Often Attracts Those with Intimacy Issues

There are situations whereby persons may seek out romantic partners but be emotionally unable to handle the pressures of relationships once formed. These types of individuals may have problems with intimacy and/or fear vulnerability. Internet infidelity indicates that a surfer might be developed enough emotionally to find a partner but perhaps not developed enough to be intimate and open in the relationship with that partner. "He or she might be partially separated, incompletely individuated or mostly undifferentiated. Separation begins with the realization that one is a separate person from mother and eventually from all others. Individuation develops as a child or adult finally assumes and places value on their own individual characteristics" (Mahler et al, 1975, Shaw, 1997, p. 31).

Schnarch (1991) states in **The Sexual Crucible** that motivation without differentiation leads to more affairs than "marital reconstruction" (p. 371). Basically, it is difficult for marriage to compete with the Internet. He states that the level of differentiation is an important determinant of the likelihood of it emerging in Internet infidelity. The impact of the infidelity is usually multisystemic, offering the surfer: "(1) defiance of feeling controlled and dominated by the spouse; (2) gratification of the desire to punish, deprive, hurt or get one up on the spouse; (3) avoidance of intimacy in the marriage while appearing to seek (or find) it on the Internet, and (4) use of the affair as a strategic buffer in the marriage and vice versa" (Schnarch, 1991, p. 367).

He believes that at low levels of differentiation, monogamy results from "reciprocal extortion of sexual exclusivity" (p. 372). This lose-lose contact fertilizes common unresolved autonomy issues that bloom into control fights and rebellious affairs. In highly differentiated couples, "the monogamy is based on two unilateral commitments for which partners owe each other nothing (except perhaps respect). The covenant is not made to the partner but rather to oneself, with the partner as witness and secondary beneficiary" (Schnarch, 1991, p. 372).

Cyber-Infidelity Regulates Anxiety

In any relationship, anxiety may arise as the individuals attempt to balance their need for closeness with their need for autonomy (Bowen, 1978). The greater the fusion of the couple, the more difficult the task of finding a stable balance satisfying to both. The resulting anxiety over regulating closeness and distance can result in triangulation. Triangulation involves a situation where emotional energy is invested in a third person, place, or thing. This investment of energy could involve work, golf, a child, an affair, or the Internet. The Internet may provide companionship, sexual fulfillment, tenderness and/or adventure. In this sort of triangulation, there is a tacit or covert agreement (sometimes even overt) by the couple to manage their anxiety by means of the Internet (Bowen, 1978).

The main attraction of the Internet is the whole notion of emotional contact without risk, exposure or being known. This is accomplished because the cyber-affair offers romantic contact while keeping "the partner from becoming a pivotal figure in one's life" (Schnarch, 1997, p.17). Shaw (1997) believes that it is possible that the cyber-affair is resultant from the couple's underdeveloped relational skills. Their poor survival patterns help them avoid confronting their loneliness and other issues in the relationship because they can consciously withdraw from each other at any time. The call of the Internet so as to avoid confronting disappointment and conflict can be irresistible.

Cyber-Infidelity Becomes a Source of Communication

The Internet can decrease the chance of the surfer to share meaning with his or her spouse. It can prevent clear, direct, person-centered communication. Instead of communicating feelings to one's spouse, the surfer tends to transfer his or her emotions on to the user(s) in cyber-space. Internet infidelity can be a result of the couple's inability to communicate feelings or needs to one another. It also can indicate that the couple does not have the verbal skills to solve problems together, or be able to accommodate to one another's needs or interests.

Cyber-Infidelity Addiction

Young (1999) defines Internet addiction as an impulse-control disorder, which does not involve an intoxicant. He found that serious relationship problems were reported by fifty-three percent of the cyber-addicts surveyed. Addicts gradually spend less time with the people in their lives in exchange for solitary time in front of the computer. Marriages appear to be the most affected as Internet use interferes with the marital and family responsibilities and obligations. In these cases, individuals may form on-line relationships, which over time can replace time spent with the spouse and/or children. The addicted spouse tends to socially isolate him or herself and may refuse to engage in typical events once enjoyed by the couple such as going out to dinner, traveling, or seeing a movie. Instead, they prefer on-line companions (Young, 1999). The ability to carry out romantic and sexual relationships on-line further then deteriorates the stability of the real life couple. As the spouse exerts more pressure on the surfer to interact, the surfer may continue to emotionally and socially withdraw from the marriage, exerting more effort to maintain the recently discovered on-line "lovers."

Therapeutic Considerations

Couples who come for therapy with the issue of Internet infidelity are experiencing problems in their relationship. They have attempted many solutions, which have been unsuccessful. Once the infidelity is out in the open, couples tend to feel ambivalent, harboring both negative and positive feelings toward the person, thing or situation. They also tend to experience combinations of devastation, hurt, betrayal, loss of self-esteem, mistrust, suspicion, fear, anger, distrust and blame. At times extreme responses may occur such as physical abuse or suicide attempts. In some cases, the spouse begins to doubt his or her judgment and even sanity, as a strange form of "gaslighting" occurs where the non-surfer spouse may question the validity of his or her complaints, feeling that, "after all the cyber-relationship is not really real." The term "Gaslighting" has been coined as a metaphor for the "head games" which occurred in the classic movie *Gaslight,* starring Charles Boyer and Ingrid Bergman. In the film, the husband systematically attempts to drive his wife mad by having the gaslights flicker and convincing his wife that she is imagining these events. It is only after the intervention of a Scotland Yard detective that her perceptions are validated and she realizes the full implications of her husband's plot to deceive her. What sometimes occurs when an affair is uncovered is that the accused attempts to convince his or her spouse that s/he has imagined many of the incidents and/or misinterpreted the evidence. There is not only an attempt to conceal with regard to gaslighting but an attempt to falsify information as well Maheu & Subotnik, 2001).

It is at this point that the gaslighting begins to become destructive, as more and more evidence of the affair is met with more assertions of the spouse's "wild imagination." One might recall that Sullivan & Swick (1968) defined reality as that which can be consensually validated. In the case of a denied affair, the only person who could possibly validate one's perceptions will not confirm what the individual "knows" s/he heard or saw. As a matter of fact, s/he is, at times, told that s/he is "hearing things" or imagining them, reinforcing the notion s/he might actually be "losing his or her mind." Often in the initial stages of the Internet infidelity, the non-surfer spouse may become suspicious of the surfer's time spent on the Internet and the resulting dismissal of other areas of his or her life. Frequently the surfer becomes edgy, short with the children, and generally seems preoccupied. This may cause the non-surfer spouse to become suspicious of his or her suspicions and discount them, only to experience them again when the surfer spouse withdraws or spends time on the computer. The non-surfer spouse often feels like s/he is on an emotional rollercoaster.

Evaluation

According to Cooper et al (1999), the therapist needs to first determine to what extent is the surfer's interaction on the Internet. Access, affordability and anonymity provided by the Internet could transform simpler, more common relational difficulties into more complex and serious troubles (Cooper et al, 1999). Once the assessment of the individual's or couple's on-line activities is accomplished, detailed information about the meanings and effects of the activities could be explored. The therapist could examine how many hours are spent on-line, what the level of direct activity is on the Internet, what type of infidelity, and how severe it is. It is also helpful to examine the intrapsychic roots of their behavior as well as current life circumstances that maintain it. Cooper, Putnam, Planchon, & Boies (1999) found that the amount of time spent on-line in sexual activities was highly correlated with the degree to which life problems were reported (see also Maheu & Subotnik, 2001b).

In addition, it would be helpful if the therapist explored also the intimate and sexual part of the couple's relationship (Schneider, 2002 in Cooper, 2002). In many cases, the surfer spouse has substituted cyber-sex for sex with his or her partner. Many spouses report that the surfer spouse had withdrawn his sexuality, intimacy and attention from the family. It is important to also explore gender differences in terms of the meanings and reasons given by the couple for Cyber-Infidelity. It is probably true that more men visit pornography sites; whereas more women visit chat rooms. Women tend to be more relational in their interactions and thus would pursue Cyber-Relationships more so than Cyber-Sex, although one may easily lead to the other (Maheu & Subotnik, 2001; Young, 2001).

Crisis Intervention

Infidelity often presents itself in the midst of crisis, with the participants experiencing emotions that seem overwhelming and out of control. The first step then is providing an emergency response. "Until the infidelity is revealed, the marriage and the therapy are merely subterfuge" (Pittman & Pittman-Wagers, 1995, p. 308). It is helpful if the therapist can provide a calm, safe setting in which the surfer and the spouse can sit down facing each other and examine what has occurred. The therapist conveys confidence that the couple will be able to accomplish this. The therapist also communicates to the couple that people can and do work through infidelity and that it does not necessarily signal the end of the relationship. In so doing, the couple can see that there are options and that drastic measures may not be necessary. "Optimism about infidelity requires the therapist to get everyone to focus on the behavior, which is controllable, rather than the emotions, which seems overwhelming and out of control" (Pittman & Pittman-Wagers, 1995, p. 311).

Loss of Self-Esteem

Cyber-infidelity chips away at the partner's self-esteem (Spring, 1996). S/he simply cannot compete with the "perfect" fantasy person. In therapy one wife wondered, "When he closes his eyes when we make love, what is thinking or visualizing? Is he picturing his cyber-sex goddess or is he thinking about me in my chubby body?" She reported that these thoughts limited her abilities to respond sexually to him.

Facing the Trauma of the Act: It IS a "Big Deal!"

Many surfer spouses do not feel that cyber-infidelity is a "big deal." In fact, the surfer spouse may deny that cyber-infidelity is an affair. S/he may feel that there was no "real" body contact that took place and that they did not actually engage in sex with the person. The spouses, on the other hand, often feel traumatized and along with feeling hurt and angry often worry about escalation of the cyber-sex into "real" contact and do consider the act as adultery and "cheating." There is some basis to their fears as Cooper et al (1999) and Cooper et al (2000) point out, accessing sex on the Internet has the potential to escalate preexisting sex addiction as well as to create new disorders.

It is crucially important for therapists not to underestimate the adverse consequences of the cyber-sex behavior. Some common mistakes made by therapists in these situations are to (1) encourage the partner to be more accepting of the surfer spouses' activities, (2) to label the surfer spouse as having sexual disinterest, (3) to believe that the behavior is not "really" sex, and/or (4) not to assess the meaning of the behavior for both spouses.

Loss of the Cyber-Lover

Loss of the cyber-lover is another issue at this time. Over the numerous e-mails, the cyber-person has become an important confidante in the surfer's life and the abrupt cessation of this relationship (which must happen if the marriage is to go forward) can cause much pain and sorrow. It is imperative that the surfer stops the behavior, both the infidelity and the lying. Anything that is deliberately hidden from a partner (whether it is the fact of being involved in an on-line affair or the specific of the on-line interactions) creates an emotional distance that can present a serious problem that is difficult to overcome. This decision to stop the Internet infidelity is best if it arises from the couple and not be a dictum of the therapist. It is also important that before continuing in the therapy that the surfer and the spouse affirm their commitment to the marriage.

Dealing with Underlying Issues

Engaging both spouses in an examination process is an important step toward dealing with Internet infidelity. To make sense of the infidelity, it is helpful if the partners explore the secrets in their relationship, what they mean and why they feel that hiding a portion of the self is necessary. The partners need to explore unresolved issues (if any) that fuel intellectual power struggles and relentless transference behaviors—both current and historical. In this way they can reclaim their projections. "The ultimate challenge of integrity is to be fully and uninhibitedly one self with one's partner rather than on-line with a stranger" (Shaw, 1997, p. 33).

It is important for the surfer spouse to examine issues of self-presentation (i.e. presenting yourself the way you want to be seen rather than how you actually are) when considering the merits of Internet infidelity (Schnarch, 1997). Does the surfer presents him/her self differently on the Internet from his/ her "real" relationship? Why does the surfer have difficulty showing that side of his/her self in the relationship? What are the surfer's needs that are met in the cyber-relationship that are not met in the marital relationship? How can the non-surfer spouse help to create an atmosphere of teamwork and safety so that honesty can prevail?

Build Communication

Cybersex takes the surfer partner away form his or her partner in terms of sexuality, attention, emotion and communication. It is also important to consider these effects on the children. For example, it is probably true that the surfer spouse is less available to spend time with his or her children, and in extreme cases, there might be a failure to fulfill family responsibilities (see Schneider, 2000b). One fifteen year client came into therapy very distraught reporting that "she had just learned her father was visiting porn sites. She had gone on the computer after he had used it and went into the history menu.

The focus of the therapy should be on empowerment and team building. This occurs through communication. There is a focus on the behaviors and communications that permit each member of the marital unit to earn each other's trust and respect. Anger must be diffused through healthy ventilation within the sessions and in the couple's home life. Guilt must be addressed, both the guilt of the surfer about what s/he has done and that of the nonparticipating spouse about what s/he may have contributed to the breakdown of the couple's system. At this point, the therapist could help the couple resolve their intensely ambivalent feelings about each other so that the marriage can go forward (Nichols, 1988).

Restoration of open communication and deepening of understanding of the current meaning or meanings of the cyber-affair are crucial. This may include determining what the partners know and what they wish to know about the affair, as well as the meaning it holds for each (Nichols, 1988, p. 193). Restoration of communication also includes dealing with what is known and acknowledged by both spouses, what is (was) the meaning of the interaction on the Internet to each of the marital partners and their marriage, and a damage control assessment.

In this phase, the therapist could emphasize changing the rules of communication, taking great care to ensure that both partners feel heard and validated. A way to do so is by filtering out several troublesome kinds of communications, such as blame (attributing bad intentions or bad traits to another or oneself), invalidation (undercutting the other person's confidence in his or her own feelings and perceptions), stalemating (closing down the possibilities for the relationship or either partner to change, and vagueness (general words or phrases that lend themselves to misinterpretations or misunderstandings) (O'Hanlon & Hudson, 1994, p. 161).

Once the couple's communication improves, it is important for them to recognize that trust may remain as an issue, regardless of the understanding of the meaning of the infidelity involvement. At some point in the therapy, it is important and helpful if the couple can create a ritual to put the past Internet infidelity in perspective. They could write out their feelings in a notebook and then perhaps include some of the e-mail symbolic of the affair. They can place the materials in shoebox and then bury the shoebox in their backyard—a symbolic burying of the past if you will. Couples should design the ritual themselves and they should decide when it should occur. The only rule is that once they have buried the past, they cannot dig it up again symbolically meaning that they may no longer discuss the Internet infidelity.

Rebuilding Marital Trust

In the initial stages of therapy, it is suggested that simple solutions be considered. Love Addicts Anonymous suggest moving the computer to an open area, not using the Internet, using the computer only for planned, specified tasks, being on line when family members are around, adding Internet control tools, arranging for some sort of accountability if there is Internet access at work (Delmonico, Griffin & Berg, 2002, in Cooper, 2002).

Lusterman (1998) believes that honesty is the necessary prelude to trust and that trust is the prelude to intimacy. Internet infidelity often happens inside the couple's home and the surfer's behavior is centralized around the computer, a tool that may also be used for non-romantic purposes such as business or home finances. In this sense the betrayal of the marriage may seem more intense as the non-surfer may feel that s/he is sleeping with the cyber-partner in their marital home so to speak. However, each time the surfer approaches the computer for a legitimate reason. It may trigger feelings of suspicion and jealousy for the spouse. The therapist can help the couple to evaluate how the computer will be used at home so that they can establish reasonable ground rules such as supervised computer use or moving the computer into a public area of the family home until a stronger trust base is built (Young, 1999). The surfer spouse must facilitate trust in the partner and the partner has to work on believing that there is a commitment to the marriage.

It is important to help the spouses understand the motives leading up to the Internet infidelity. The surfer may rationalize the behavior as just fantasy, typed words on a screen, or say that cyber-sex is not cheating because of the lack of physical contact. This is a form of "gaslighting" and can serve to "crazy-make" the non-surfer spouse because his or her reality is being invalidated. It is important for the therapist to focus on ways for the surfer to take responsibility for his/her actions (Young, 1999). In so doing, the therapist should take a benevolent stance rather than a judgmental one.

Here the therapist could help the couple evaluate how the Internet infidelity has hurt the relationship and help formulate relationship enhancing goals that can assist them in renewing their commitment so that intimacy can grow once again. The therapist can ask about the couple's activity pre-Internet cyber-relationship. How did they have fun then? What were the types of activities the couple did before the Internet came into their lives? The couple could develop a couple contract where they spend time together as a couple where they are free of distraction and where they can be honest, loving and caring toward each other.

Constructing New Stories

The stories we create about our lives and relationships both arise from and shape our experiences. Our many life stories are both our creations and our creators. They are the principal way that each of us participates with others in the making and remaking of ourselves as social beings. When partners are at impasse in their relationship, their individual and couple stories have become predominantly narratives of limitation. The past is experienced as fixed and foreclosed rather than in flux and open (Atwood, 1997; Roth & Chasin, 1994).

During this phase the therapist can help the couple become more aware that they have a choice in change. They can see that that there are numerous scripts to choose from. Change requires at least a two-sided perspective, and a therapist may seek to construct a relational definition by assisting the couple in uncovering two or more complementary definitions of the problem. Here, complementary questions can be introduced to help deconstruct the dominant explanation and to assist couples in achieving a relational or double description of the problem. This double description then provides the source of new responses (Atwood et al).

Future focus enables the couple to visualize their relationship in which the Internet infidelity is no longer an issue and the couple feels empowered and confident that they possess skills necessary to solve other problems. By asking questions about future trends and choices, the therapist is making that future more real and more stable.

Ritual for a Fresh Start

At the end of the therapy, a ritual for a fresh start may be helpful. At this time, couples can choose a new anniversary date when they recommit to each other. They can rewrite their marital vows and hold a ceremony where they "remarry" each other. They can purchase new wedding rings. "Along with restating their commitment to each other and to the relationship, they can write down their future relationship vision. This becomes their future image, the template for their relationship" (Atwood et al).

Conclusions

Internet infidelity is a new and increasing problem couples are bringing into therapy. In these cases, the therapist's role in helping the couple is first to explore the therapist's own feelings about Internet infidelity—does the therapist consider it a breach of the couple contract? Does the therapist consider it infidelity? Next it is helpful to evaluate the extent of the infidelity, and to provide a crisis intervention for the couple. Here the couple can explore their feelings about the Internet infidelity, ultimately putting it in perspective. Once there is a calm and safe setting, the therapist could examine how the Internet provided the couple with an excuse not to relate to one another. Feelings of mistrust, loss of self-esteem, and the hurt and anger could be explored and validated. For the spouse, Internet infidelity is a big deal. Once the couple is able to move beyond the infidelity, the therapist could work on building the couple's communication and trust with each other, assisting them to construct new stories about their future. At the end of therapy the couple should feel empowered in their skills and enhanced as team—stronger for having conquered the affair.

Joan D. Atwood, Ph.D., LMFT, LCSW & Conchetta Gallo, Ph.D., LMFT

Internet infidelity has become a growing trend faced by many couples therapists. Unlike traditional infidelity, Internet infidelity often occurs in one's home or office, sometimes with no real thought of looking for an affair. Like traditional infidelity, Internet infidelity could be an indicator that there are issues in the relationship that need to be addressed. This paper focused on this new phenomenon, examined some of the factors often associated with this type of infidelity and explored some therapeutic considerations.

References

Atwood, Joan D. (ed.) (1997). *Challenging family therapy situations: Perspectives in social construction.* Springer: New York.

Atwood, J. D. et al. Extramarital affairs and constructed meaning: A social constructionist therapeutic approach. *The American Journal of Family Therapy, 25*(1), 55-75.

Cooper, A., Putnam, D., Planchon, L., & Boies, S. (1999). On-line sexual compulsivity: Getting tangled in the net. *Sexual Addiction and Compulsivity, 6,* 2, 79-201.

Cooper, A., Delmonico, D., & Burg, R. (2000). Cybersex users, abusers, and complusives. New findings and implications. *Sexual Addiction & Compusivity, 7,* 1, 5-30.

Cooper, A. (2002). Sex and the internet: A Guidebook for clinicians. Brunner-Routledge:New York.

Glover, C. & Redshaw, I.B. (1996). *Locus of control among internet users: A preliminary investigation of the internet* [On-line]. Available: http://pegasus.cc.ucf.edu/~cwg65985/results.html

Greenfield, D. N. & Cooper, A. (1994). *Crossing the line—On line.* [On-line]. Available: http://www.shpm.com/articles/cyber_romance/sexcross.html.

Hamman, R. B. (1996). The role of fantasy in the construction of the on-line other: A selection of interviews and participant observations from cyber-space. [On-line]. Available: http://www.socio.demon.co.uk/fantasy.html

Hudson-O'Hanlon, W., & O'Hanlon-Hudson, P. (1994). Co-authoring a love story: Solution-oriented marital therapy. In M. F. Hoyt (Ed.). *Constructive therapies.* New York: Guilford Press.

Humphrey, F. G. (1987). Treating Extramarital sexual relationships in sex and couples therapy. In G. R. Weeks & L. Hof (Eds.) *Integrating sex and marital therapy: A clinical guide.* New York: Brunner/Mazel.

Katz, J. E. & Aspden, P. (1998). Friendship Formation in Cyber-space Analysis of a National Survey of Users. [On-line]. Available: http://

Leiblum, S.R. (1997). Sex and the net: Clinical implications. *Journal of Sex Education and Therapy, 22*(1), 15-20.

Lusterman, D. (1998). *Infidelity: A survival guide.* New York: MJF Books.

Maheu, M., Subotnik, R. (2001*). Infidelity on the internet.* CA.: Sourcebook Trade.

Mahler, M. S., Pine, F., & Bergman, A. (1975). *The psychological birth of the human infant: Symbiosis and individuation.* New York: Basic Books.

New York Times. October 23, 2000.

Nichols, W. C. (1988). *Marital therapy: An integrative approach.* New York: Guilford Press.

Parks, M. R. & Floyd, K. (1996). Making friends in cyber-space. *Journal of Communication, 46*(1), 80-97.

Pittman, F. S. & Pittman Wagers, T. (1995). Crises of infidelity. In N. Jacobson & A. Gurman (Eds.) *Clinical handbook of couple therapy.* New York: Guilford Press.

Quittner, J. (1997). Divorce Internet style. *Time,* April 14, p. 72.

Roth, S., & Chasin, R. (1994). Entering one another's worlds of meaning and imagination: Dramatic enactment and narrative couple therapy. In M. F. Hoyt (Ed.). *Constructive therapies.* New York: Guilford Press.

Schnarch, D. (1991). *Constructing the sexual crucible: An integration of sexual and marital therapy.* New York: W. W. Norton & Co.

Schnarch, D. (1997). Sex, intimacy, and the internet. *Journal of Sex Education and Therapy, 22*(1), 15-20.

Schneider, J. (2000a). A qualitative study of cyber-sex participants: Gender differences, recovery issues, and implications for therapists, *Sexual Addiction and Compulsivity. 7,* 249-278.

Schneider, J. (2000b). Effects of cyber-sex, addiction on the family: Results of a survey. *Sexual Addiction and Compulsivity, 7,* 1, 31-58.

Sempsey, J. (1997). *Psyber Psychology: A Literature review Pertaining to the Psycho/Social Aspects of Multi-User Dimensions in Cyber-space.* [On-line]. Available: http://journal.tinymush.org/v2n1/sempsey.html.

Shaw, J. (1997) Treatment rationale for Internet infidelity. *Journal of Sex Education and Therapy, 22*(1), 29-34.

Suler, J. (1997). *The final showdown between in-person and cyber-space relationships.* [On-line]. Available: http://www.rider.edu/users/suler/psycyber/showdown.html.

Suler, J. (1998). *Mom, Dad, Computer (Transference reactions to computers).* [On-line]. Available: http://www.rider.edu/users/suler/psycyber/comptransf.html

Sullivan, H., Swick, H. (1968). *The interpersonal theory of psychiatry.* New York: W. W. Norton & Co.

Thompson, A.T. (1983). Extramarital sex: A review of research literature. *Journal of Sex Research, 19*(1), 1-22.

Turkle, S. (1995). *Life on the screen: Identity in the age of the Internet.* New York: Simon and Schuster.

Vaughan, P. (1998). *On-line Affairs*. [On-line]. Available: http:// www. vaughan-vaughan.com/com010.html.

Young, K. (1996). *Internet addiction: The emergence of a new clinical disorder*. Paper presented at the 104th annual meeting of the American Psychological Association, August 11, 1996. Toronto, Canada.

Young, K. (1999). Internet addiction: Symptoms, evaluation and treatment. In L. VandeCreek & T. Jackson (Eds.). *Innovations in clinical practice: A source book*. Sarasota, FL: Professional Resource Press.

Young, K., O'Mara, J., & Buchanan, J. (1999). *Cybersex and infidelity on-line: implications for evaluation and treatment*. Poster presented at the 107th annual meeting of the American Psychological Association. August 21, 1999. Hynes Convention Center.

Young, K. (2001). Tangled in a web: *Understanding cybersex from fantasy to addiction*. MA.: First Books Library.

CHAPTER 7

Pornography
and Its Effects on Relationships

Sarah Alvi
Kathleen O'Rourke
Saadia Z. Yunus

Joan D. Atwood, Ph.D., LMFT, LCSW & Conchetta Gallo, Ph.D., LMFT

Introduction

Pornography has become a widespread epidemic with the availability of resources that the Internet provides. It no longer includes dirty magazines that someone needs to frantically hide under the bed, but it is readily available at the tip of anyone's fingertips and can be looked at without having to leave behind a trace. In the twenty-first century, when the world can be accessed at our own pace, in the comfort of our own homes, and without anyone having to know, it is no shock that Internet pornography has become a hot topic.

Once ashamed of secret fetishes and fantasies, one can simply type these keywords into a search engine and realize that their fetishes and fantasies are not so secret nor are they alone in having them. With this influx of streaming pornography, social networks, fetish chat rooms, and so on, the modern world of relationships and monogamy must redefine their boundaries and rules for what is acceptable and what is not.

In January 2000 alone, 17.5 million surfers visited porn sites from their homes (C/Net, 2001) and an estimated 50% of all Internet traffic now is related to sex sites (McNair, 2002). In 2006, 13% of website visits in America were to sex-related sites (Albright, 2008). With statistics like these, it is no longer safe to assume that masturbation is being kept to a minimum in a bathroom with a Playboy magazine. Many of these sites are interactive and include video and non-video chat rooms for members to discuss their sexual preferences. So, the question that needs to be asked today is, where do we draw the line? How much room can a relationship make for Internet pornography without the members feeling that they are no longer in a monogamous relationship? Does watching pornography and partaking in these chat rooms necessarily mean that one is not monogamous?

Schneider (2000) surveyed the effects of cybersex on the family, and the results of her research study showed that cybersex caused much distress on the partner due to the amount of lies the partner told as well as various other reasons. The partner felt a sense of betrayal and abandonment, closely identifying with those partners that have been cheated on with real women or men in person. The fact that these partners were using pornography and not engaging with real people did not make a difference in their feelings of hurt.

Schneider (2000) also reported a significant decrease in the couple's sex life that coincided with the cybersex addiction. The spouses that no longer needed to suffice their sexual appetite with their partner due to their Internet outlet were not going unnoticed. Among 68% of the couples, one or both had lost interest in relational sex: 52.1% of addicts bad decreased interest in sex with their spouse, as did 34% of partners. So, although the lack of interest in sex with the partner was something that many partners shared as well, many more addicts were no longer interested in being intimate with their spouses.

The Internet was providing an alternative method to those spouses that were not able to get what they need sexually from their spouses. It allows for them to get what they need without having to leave their house or even meet people in real life. This is not always the case, but the population that is being consulted for this particular study is not having extramarital affairs outside of the computer. Knowing that one can come home after an exhausting day at work and not have to worry about meeting their partner's sexual needs that night because they are helping themselves with images of women or men that do not seem to be real and are not having what one might call a "real" affair might seem as if it would enhance the couple's sex lives for when they did have sex. This study is showing that the opposite result is the case due to the lack of interest the addicted spouses now have towards their partners and vice versa. Internet pornography was not an alternate method to their partner at this point, but a primary source of where they were going to comfort their sexual needs, leaving their partners to feel jealous and betrayed. The partners reported on feelings of jealousy that they will never look like the porn stars that their partner's internet pornography consists of, therefore making them feel inadequate and subpar to them. (Schneider, 2000) These types of feelings can contribute to the addict's sex-seeking behavior on the Internet because their partners no longer feel adequate in the bedroom.

When Internet addiction occurs, making room for it is very hard in the relationship because the porn is no longer there to enhance the relationship sexually. The partner is not looking to fulfill one particular fantasy from the Internet pornography; they are satisfying all of their sexual needs from the cybersex, therefore no longer needing a partner in that area. This does not contribute to the marriage or the relationship because one partner is going to feel betrayed and resentful. If the Internet addiction is not there, the question still remains, can relationships adjust to making room for some frisky behaviors on the Internet if those same behaviors are not lacking in the bedroom?

Whitty (2002) investigated community attitudes towards Internet relationships, and whether they are considered to be acts of betrayal. This study involved 1117 participants with equal numbers of males and females aged between 17 and 70. Participants were asked to what extent they considered participating in cybersex, engaging in online sexual chat, sharing online versus offline emotional information, and engaging in face-to-face sexual intercourse to be acts of infidelity. The results suggested that online romantic relationships were considered to be 'real' acts of betrayal. Additionally, some online activities, including online sexual activity, were considered to be more significant acts of betrayal than some offline acts of infidelity, such as sharing intimate information. Whitty's study therefore suggests that online actions can have significant impact regardless of the physical availability of the partners.

Whitty's and Schneider's studies both support the claim that online relationships, including pornography and cybersex, do fall under the line of infidelity. There is a broad population that will consider the use of Internet pornography as a form of cheating and many of the studies report this. Although this seems to be the popular vote, there is a small population that does not necessarily consider these activities as cheating and instead has an increased understanding for them.

Cooper, Morahan-Martin, Mathy, and Maheu (2002) studied the demographics of online sex users and how their relationships were affected. They found that there is an increased understanding amongst today's population for those who engage in online sexual activity. Significantly more than half (63.6%) of the total sample reported that their online sexual activity had not affected their relationship with their partner. However, males were significantly more likely than females to indicate that their online sexual activity had not affected their relationship with their partner (64.4% and 59.8%, respectively). Nonetheless, significantly more than half the total sample (65.3%) reported that their online sexual activity had not had a positive effect on their relationships. Males were significantly more likely than females to report their online sexual activity had not had a positive effect on their relationships.

These results are very interesting for a variety of reasons First off; men were more likely to report that their online sexual activity had not had a positive effect on their relationship. This shows that men are more understanding as significant others of online sexual activity and their partner engaging in it than females. Females seem to be more jealous and therefore are not as thrilled about their husbands or boyfriends using what the Internet has to offer in terms of sex. Men are more open to this. They do not view it as a bad thing and that their wife is cheating; they view it as an enhancing tool in their own sex life with their significant other, and therefore they report more of a positive effect on their relationship with female online sexual users.

Even with that being said, more than half the population in the sample still reported that online sexual activity did not have a positive effect on their relationship. This study did show some progression towards a more understanding population, more so than any of the other studies for sure, but there is still much hesitation about online sexual activity in today's society and it is still very taboo to look at it. Until these perceptions are challenged redefined, most of the studies will find that females feel much more strongly about Internet sexual use than men will.

Although 62.1% of adults who go online are married (U.S. Department of Commerce, 1999), 43.4% of online sexual activity users measured in the current study reported that they were married. Compared with male users of online sexual activity, females were less likely to be married (33.2% versus 45.3%), but more likely to be in committed relationships (32% versus 20.8%), but were more likely to be in committed relationships. (Cooper et al, 2002) These statistics run alongside with the results of the study, and also show some reasons of the reactions to online sexual activity for the different genders.

Looking at the results from these different studies, helps us to realize where we are in today's society when it comes to relationships and Internet pornography, and how we view both of these things in relation to one another as well as on their own. The demographic numbers show that women and men feel very different about online sexual activity. Men tend to be more understanding of their partner's internet use than women are, but men also have higher statistics in partaking in these online sexual activities, which could account for the reasons that they are more understanding about it. Most women feel that it is a form of cheating and infidelity and is uncomfortable with their significant other's usage, especially when the usage goes from occasional to cybersex addiction.

Some studies also showed the reasons behind the online sexual activity usage as being more than just a source of masturbation. Underwood and

Findlay (2004) explored Internet relationships that were extra-dyadic with their primary relationships. The participants in this study were those who did not just have a sexual Internet relationship, these were relationships of various types, ones which were solely people they talked to over the Internet. Underwood and Finlay looked into some of the reasons for why these Internet relationships occurred, and these were the results: Of the 95% of respondents who answered the question 'To what extent are you satisfied with your online relationship?' nearly two-thirds (63%) reported that they found their online relationship to be satisfying and meaningful. A quarter (25%) neither agreed nor disagreed. A small number (11%) of respondents disagreed or strongly disagreed. In contrast, of the 84% of respondents who answered the question 'To what extent are you satisfied with your primary relationship?' most respondents (75%) remained neutral, disagreed, or strongly disagreed. Only a very small number (6%) of respondents strongly agreed that they found their primary relationship satisfying.

Of the 31 respondents who reported dissatisfaction with their primary relation-ship, 8 (26%) reported that there were constant unresolved problems; 10 (32%) reported sexual dissatisfaction; 5 (16%) reported different child-rearing beliefs; 4 (13%) had been recently relocated away from family and friends; 6 (19%) reported financial problems; 10 (32%) reported that they do not communicate about important issues; and 11 (35%) reported that their primary relationship was in a rut. (Underwood & Findlay, 2004)

These findings conclude that many people do not go looking for an Internet relationship without there being some kind of problem in their primary relationship. Their Internet relationship does not always bring about a sexual nature; some people are looking for a person to hear them out when things are wrong in their primary relationship.

This may be the reason that many women do call online sexual activity a form of infidelity and men do not. Women imagine these scenarios where the sexual relationship will stem into a more meaningful one. Especially in today's day and age, their own relationship with their significant other might have started that way and therefore making them feel extra threatened. Many relationships today started over the Internet, so it is understandable why some people might feel that online sexual activity is a form of cheating if their own relationship had begun with the same story.

With statistics as high as over 50% of Internet sites visited are those of a sexual nature, this is not an issue that can be ignored. It is an issue that should be addressed in today's couples. Reasons behind the Internet use should be revealed to both partners, making them feel safe and trusted. If the Internet use is of a minimal nature, and is there to enhance the couple's own sexual behaviors, or even to have that alone time, I think that many more couples would be open to that and not as threatened. It is the over-usage of these sexual websites, the bordering of sexual addiction, and the formation of actual Internet relationships, that require partners of these users to feel a lot more betrayed and hurt and view these behaviors as a form of infidelity.

This research paper is looking at online sexual users, frequent and infrequent, and viewing how the effects of the usage are different based on the individual, marital status, and religiosity. Findings of different populations and their views will contribute to the tendencies of a variety of Internet pornography users.

(Saadia)

Pornography—Facts and Figures

With its "Triple A engine" of accessibility, affordability, and anonymity via the World Wide Web, online pornography is attracting a larger audience than ever before (Cooper, 2000). In the past, if anyone wanted to access sexually explicit materials, he/she would need to physically go to an adult video store or other such locations to obtain them, whereas the Internet has made sexually explicit material available from the comfort of one's home. A staunch statistic reveals just how much easier the Internet has made accessing pornography: in January 2000 alone, 17.5 million surfers visited pornographic sites from their homes (CNet, 2001). With the ease of the Internet, a vast amount of information is available at the touch of a button, whether it encompasses the area of jobs, education, hobbies, etc. However, out of all that is available via the Internet, sexually explicit materials are the most viewed subject matter (Cooper, Galbreath, & Becker, 2004).

Now, with pornographic material easily accessible and in high demand, marriage and family therapists are encountering clients with internet-related problems more than ever before. Such problems include cybersex addiction, pornography use that is interfering in a couple's relationship, a couple on the brink of divorce because of an online affair, a mother concerned about her teenager's viewing of pornography, and more. Marriage and family therapists need to be well-versed in the technological advancement of pornography as well as the impact that it has on the wide array of individuals, couples, and families who will come in for therapy.

Gender and Sexual Identity Differences

When comparing those who access porn online, research has found that 86% of males reported viewing pornography online versus 59% of females (Cooper, 2000). In a more recent study, it was 75% of males and 41% of females who downloaded porn (Albright, 2008). These statistics reveal that the majority of those who view pornographic material online are males. One specific gender issue that is important to note is that a large majority of those dealing with sexual addictions and compulsive pornography use via the Internet are married, heterosexual males (Cooper, Delmonico, & Burg, 2000).

Gender differences are also found when considering the reason behind viewing pornography online. The majority of women who view pornography report their reasoning to be improved sexual performance with their partners, including viewing pornography together to enhance arousal. Men, on the other hand, view pornography to enhance arousal when they are unaccompanied, which often leads to secrecy from their partners (Albright, 2008). Because of this position of secrecy, the vast amount of research on pornography focuses primarily on men as the viewers and women as the partners who discover their partner's pornography consumption.

With regard to sexual orientation, research shows that gays are only 20% as likely to access porn as straights, and bisexuals are 50% as likely to view erotic images intentionally. However, those who reported compulsive use of pornography were more likely to be single and lesbian/gay or bisexual than straight (Albright, 2008).

Positive Effects of Pornography

Although a vast majority of research shows the negative impact of pornography on individuals and couples, there is some research that shows that it can have positive effects as well. With regard to individuals, the perceived positive effects of pornography are the following: producing sexual arousal, giving new ideas for sexual behavior, producing a feeling of relaxation, providing a sexual outlet where they do not have to deal with others, and a risk-free choice from sexually-transmitted diseases (Baltazar, Helm, Jr., McBride, Hopkins, & Stevens, Jr., 2010). Perceived positive effects were the same for males and females.

When positive effects on couples are considered, many couples view sexually erotic images together to enhance their sexual repertoire when routine and boredom take the place of excitement and enjoyment (Philaretou, Maoufouz, & Allen, 2005). These couples use pornography as a relational sexual stimulant.

Oftentimes, this occurs when women discover their partner's porn consumption and, instead of demanding their partners to quit altogether, they communicate to their partners a "willingness to learn and adopt pornographic scripts as part of generating intimacy and a sense of togetherness in the relationship" (Benjamin & Tlusten, 2010, p. 616). These women view their partner's interest in pornography somewhat similar to a hobby and decide they would rather be involved than excluded from their partner's extracurricular activities. "Given the image of heterosexual togetherness as based on a preference for joint activities, joint consumption of pornography is one safe path towards relationship enhancement" (Benjamin & Tlusten, 2010, p. 613). However, mutual consumption is not a common occurrence, since the vast majority of situations involve one partner viewing erotic images alone and oftentimes without the knowledge of the other partner.

Negative Effects of Pornography

The internet, although positive in countless ways, can allow for compulsive pornography use, which leads to numerous psychosocial problems, such as relationship and family breakups, depression, anxiety, isolation, and a tendency to indulge in sexually deviant behaviors (Cooper, Delmonico, Griffin-Shelley, & Mathy, 2004). This compulsive pornography use, or cybersex addiction, has been defined as viewing pornography for more than 11 hours a week. However, the amount of time that pornography viewing takes is not the only aspect that causes negative results. Research shows that since pornography use takes up an extreme amount of effort, energy, and time, it can often lead to depression, anxiety, and interpersonal problems (Cooper, Delmonico, & Burg, 2000)

A comprehensive study focusing on the effects of pornography on the individual found that "exposure to pornographic material puts one at increased risk for developing sexually deviant tendencies, committing sexual offences, experiencing difficulties in one's intimate relationships, and accepting the rape myth (that women cause rape)" (Oddone-Paolucci, Genuis, and Violato, 2000). These negative effects on the individual are consistently discussed throughout the literature on the topic of pornography.

When one's partner is addicted to cybersex, the individual, upon discovering it, feels hurt, betrayed, rejected, abandoned, devastated, lonely, ashamed, isolated, humiliated, jealous, angry, and low in self-esteem (Schneider, 2000). What is even more hurtful than the cybersex itself is the secrecy and lying that the partner has been involved in. Poor self-esteem develops from evaluating oneself based on pornographic images, resulting in a negative view, and feeling "hopeless about being able to compete" with those on screen (p.31).

Another aspect of the negative outcomes of pornography focuses on the negative message that pornography sends about women. Pornography has the ability to "shape the attitudes and conduct of its audience in ways that are injurious to women", which is the harm hypothesis posed by anti-porn feminists (Eaton, 2007, p. 677). By displaying women in sadomasochistic and other subjugated ways, this specific type of pornography, termed "inegalitarian pornography", further deepens the divide between male and female equality in society.

Impact on Couples

A vast amount of research on pornography takes a linear focus in that it discusses the impact pornography has on the individual, whether it is the individual who engages in pornography use or the partner who is affected by the other's use of it. Where the research is lacking is when it comes to a systemic focus on the impact of pornography, focusing on its impact on couples and families. The reason for the importance of this is that the "impact of sexually explicit material is felt by entire family systems, not to mention communities and corporate circles" (Manning, 2006, p. 138).

Although the scope of the effects of pornography resonates through society, the systemic relationship that is affected the most is the marital dyad. A couple's relationship is based on many components, including love, togetherness, compassion, passion, friendship, and commitment. Although these components are debatable since many relationships exist without all six ingredients, it has been found that passion is a necessary ingredient of a successful relationship (Benjamin and Tlusten, 2010). It has been argued that "if passion, as one facet of the relationship, is absent, then the relationship loses its reason for being and becomes subject to dissolution" (p. 602). Situations in which such sexual passion is directed at pornographic images instead of the partner cause a divide between the couple, particularly those who are married since the marital dyad "can be easily destabilized by sexual pursuits outside the marital contract" (Manning, 2006, p. 138).

Specifically in a marriage, "internet pornography is associated with activities that can undermine marital exclusivity and fidelity" (Manning, 2006, p. 145). Partners feel betrayed when they discover that their partner has been viewing pornography, which is perceived as infidelity (Whitty, 2003). The emotional distance that is created by this online relationship is said to create a deeper divide between the couple than real-life affairs (Schneider, 2002). This situation leads to conflict between the couple, and since it is seen as a breach of trust, it takes time, and often therapy, to heal the relationship. Usually, the partner who discovers that his/her significant other is "cheating" by viewing pornography is so deeply hurt and angered that the strain on the relationship ends in a breakup. It has been found that when casual pornography becomes compulsive, it is likely to lead to the severing of ties, since cybersex addiction is "a major contributing factor to separation and divorce" for affected couples (Schneider, 2000, p. 31).

Pornography consumption also negatively affects the couples' sex lives. Couples report a decrease in relationship sex and an adverse effect on the couple's sexual relationship when one of the partners is a regular viewer of pornography (Schneider, 2000). One reason for this is that women are reluctant to have sex with their partners who watch pornography because they are afraid their partners will view them negatively and that they will be pressured to engage in undesirable sexual activities (Shaw, 1999). Another reason for the detrimental effect on relational sex is that pornography use has been found to decrease a person's sexual satisfaction with his/her partner. Men reported that it causes them to be critical of their partners' bodies and to have less desire to have sex with their partners (Albright, 2008). More specifically, those who regularly view pornography report "less satisfaction with their intimate partner and specifically with their partner's (a) affection, (b) physical appearance, (c) sexual curiosity, and (d) sexual performance" (Manning, 2006, p.142). In addition, female partners (spouses, girlfriends, fiancés) of men who regularly view pornography all report low sexual desire in their partners (Bergner & Bridges, 2002).

While women say that viewing porn causes them to view themselves negatively and to have less sex with their partners, felt intimacy of both men and women with their partners has shown to be negatively affected by pornography (Albright, 2008). Although the sexual relations were there, the women reported a decrease in sexual intimacy and closeness that existed before their partner became an avid viewer of pornographic material. They describe their partner's sexual advancements as conveying a "message of objectification as opposed to meaningful interaction" (Manning, p. 143). When either partner turns to pornographic entertainment, the intimacy of the relationship is challenged since "sexuality reflects deeper intimate processes" (Benjamin & Tlusten, 2010, p. 613).

Another negative effect is that men who view pornography display significantly more controlling behaviors in their close-knit relationships (Simmons & Lehmann, 2008). This depends on the amount of time a man spends watching pornography and also what types of pornography he is viewing. The more time a man spends viewing dehumanizing pornography, the more he is likely to be dominating and controlling in his real-life relationships with women.

Another factor that concerns men and their pornography use involves their coping skills. Because many times, men turn to pornography when they are stressed out and are unable to cope with the stresses of life, they are less likely to work on actually improving their real relationships (Cooper, Galbreath, & Becker, 2004). These men tend to manage stress by following a pattern of turning inward instead of dealing with others in all situations, including with their marriage. As a result, the intimacy in the relationship suffers.

One significant difference in the impact on couples is whether the couple is married or cohabitating. Married women tend to be considerably more troubled by a partner's online pornography use than women in dating partnerships (Bridges, Bergner, and Hesson-McInnis,

2003). Because these women view pornography as a threat to their marital bond and a breach of the marital contract of fidelity, this concept is more difficult to accept. Research may very well go along with this idea since "internet pornography consumption in a growing number of relationships may be considered incompatible with the characteristics of stable, healthy marriages", of which are fidelity and trust (Manning, 2006, p. 157). A significant statistic about married couples is that "people who report being happily married are 61% less likely to report using Internet pornography compared to survey respondents who did not report being happily married" (Stack, Wasserman, & Kern, 2004, p. 157).

Religious and Cultural Implications

Research has examined the relationship between pornography and religiosity to determine whether there is a connection, and results have been mixed. Studies suggest that religiosity serves as a protective barrier from harm, such as violence, drug abuse, crime, and alcoholism (Baltazar, et.al, 2010). When ascertaining whether religiosity serves the same protection from pornography, some results show that this is not the case and that religiosity may actually place the individual at considerable risk (Abell et. al, 2006). However, one recent study shows that religiosity may indeed be a protective factor against compulsive pornography usage since the males in the study reported using the internet about half as much as the general population of males (Baltazar, et. al, 2010).

The majority of research studying the correlation between religion and pornography focuses on Christianity. Recent studies show that with regard to conservative Christians, although many are involved in viewing pornographic material, "regular viewing was significantly lower than has been found in the general population" (Baltazar, et. al, 2010, p. 32). Other studies, however, have shown that Christians use pornography at a high rate (Levert, 2007). One reason for this is that because pornography viewing can be kept a secret from everyone else, the individual can display religiosity in public and be viewed as a religious figure without having to practice that in private (Levert, 2007). This concept may apply to religious individuals of any religious background.

An aspect that particularly relates to Christian couples is the feeling of isolation—that no other Christian is going through the same situation. What is proven to be helpful is to provide the couple with articles from religious magazines that discuss other couples going through a similar situation (White & Kimball, 2009). The concept of sin and forgiveness are also very important to religious couples dealing with a cybersex addiction, and a therapist working with such a couple should focus on these areas in order to assist the couple in the best possible way. The couples in this research study epitomized the "victim paradigm" in that they showed fear that the church members would find out about their issue, felt isolated from the community, and did not understand the context of healthy sexuality within a Christian marriage (p. 357). Oftentimes, a religious congregation ignores the pornography issue as well as the problem of cybersex addiction. This avoidance of discussing sexual issues may lead to the problem expanding in the community because it is not addressed.

As with religious men in general, it is predicted that these men are more likely to engage in solitary pornography viewing because it is more acceptable in their religion than premarital or extramarital sex (Abell et. al, 2006). Going back to the concept of sin, which is an essential component in most religions, including Christianity, Judaism, and Islam, these men choose the lesser of two evils.

With regard to cultural implications of pornography, it has been found that in Israeli heterosexual relationships, a common trend is that the male is the one who initiates the idea of pornography, whether for himself or for the couple to view together. The female, not wanting to be excluded from his sexual interests, eventually cooperate with their partner, which is "inevitable once they are unable to justify explicit rejection of pornography" (p. 614). For the sake of maintaining the quality of the relationship, these women give in to their partner's interest in pornography. Although this study was done studying the effects of pornography with Israeli women, it may be generalizable to many heterosexual relationships.

(Kathleen)

Treatment Considerations

When considering the systemic treatment of a couple struggling with pornography use, it is important to look at the impact of pornography consumption on the consumer, the consumer's partner, and the relationship itself. The research surrounding this topic focuses on male heterosexuals as the primary consumers of pornography, hence for our purposes we will assume the consumer is male and the partner is female.

Impact on Men

There is a dearth of research exploring the influence of pornography consumption on specific behaviors. Rather, substantial data has been collected identifying correlated consequences and outcomes to porn use and consumption. Correlated outcomes should not suggest causality, however. The research prior to the invention of the internet focused on repeated exposure to "standard, non-violent, commonly available" pornography (Zillman and Bryant, 1984). Researchers identified nine common consequences correlated with ongoing exposure: increased callousness towards women, trivialization of rape as a criminal offense, distorted perceptions about sex, increased appetite for increasingly bizarre pornography, devaluation of importance of monogamy, decreased satisfaction with partners sexual performance and/or attractiveness, doubts about the value of marriage, decreased desire to have children, and, finally, increased view of non-monogamous relationships as normal and natural (Zillman & Bryant, 1984, 1988b).

While this research did not approach the systemic implications of these consequences, the potential for harm to a relationship is clear: repeated exposure may alter a man's perception of his partner and perception of his current relationship. This research was conducted prior to the advent of the internet, and the subsequent explosion of availability of pornography, not only in quantity, but in increasingly diverse quality. The consequences of pornography usage as described above will only be amplified as the pervasive nature of internet pornography progresses. More men, at younger ages, are being exposed to more types of pornography. This is an area that warrants further study. Males who began exploring pornography as adolescents online in the early days of the internet bring a decade of exposure to any relationship they may approach. Do these men view women fundamentally different than men who were not raised in a culture of porn? Additionally, how are women who are raised in porn culture different from women who were not?

Joan D. Atwood, Ph.D., LMFT, LCSW & Conchetta Gallo, Ph.D., LMFT

Impact on Women

Very little research has been completed exploring the impact of porn consumption on attitudes and behaviors of female *users*. As identified previously, this is a gap in the literature. Hence, our focus here is on the impact of a partner's pornography usage on the female spouse. Bergner and Bridges (2002) identified several themes that emerged from anecdotal expressions of women posted on an internet chat room/support group who described their partners as 'heavily involved' with online non-interactive pornography. An operational definition for 'heavily involved' was not given, but we may conclude that the writings posted stemmed from a place of interpersonal distress, and that the specific quantity of consumption was, almost, irrelevant. Non-interactive pornography was defined as such that did not involve viewing another person, or being viewed by another person, chatting, or exchange of other personal information, including photos (Bergner & Bridges, p. 194).

The data reveals four significant themes in female response. First, the woman viewed discovery of the porn consumption by her partner as a traumatic event. Additionally, women report redefining their relationship, reevaluating their sense of self, and looking at their partner in a different light after experiencing the trauma. Understandably, the potential impact on a relationship is significant: a traumatic response, feelings of betrayal and loss of trust, and changes to perceptions of self and partner not only damage a relationship, but may kill it outright.

A more recent study conducted by Schneider (2000) revealed similar themes running through the expressions of partners, however, her research involved partners of diagnosed sex addicts. The congruence of reactions and overall impact suggests that it is not the characteristics of the usage (material used, frequency, duration, or type) that define relational impact, but the partners perceptions *of that usage*.

A criticism of the previously presented research is that it focuses on a somewhat clinical sample of women, specifically those who are currently experiencing interpersonal problems in conjunction with pornography usage. A study by Bergner, Bridges and Hesson-McInnis (2003) attempted to identify if the emotional themes expressed in previous research was representative of all women. They found that approximately one third of women attribute highly negative outcomes to porn usage by a partner. Additional correlates identified include increased distress surrounding usage for married women vs. dating women, and increased distress in women reporting highest levels of consumption by partners (both frequency and duration of use) (Bridges, Bergner & Hesson-McInnis, p. 13). Both of these are indicators of perceived threat to the relationship, further supporting the idea that objective consumption is not the issue, but the partner's subjective perception of the consumption, which defines parameters of distress.

Impact on Relationship of Partners/Systemic Impact

The research clearly suggests that the potential harm of ongoing exposure to, or consumption of, pornography, is relational or interpersonal in nature, rather than having some specific physiological impact on sexual functioning. Goldberg and Peterson (2008) explored the frequency of pornography as an issue in the practice of marriage and family therapists and concluded that 1) a majority of clinicians are dealing with porn usage and its systemic impact, and 2) the numbers of families affected by porn usage are increasing. As clinicians, we may beg the question: "Will there come a time in the near future where porn is a de-facto aspect of couples' dynamics?"

Treatment

Little research is available detailing therapeutic techniques, interventions or approaches for couples dealing with pornography usage of a partner. Overwhelmingly, the research suggests that regular consumption of pornography by one partner in a relationship *feels like* an affair or infidelity. As clinicians, it is important to validate the experience of the couple. This is not to suggest that all couples presenting for marital therapy where one of the partners consumes pornography should be labeled as an unfaithful relationship. The crucial indicator for this type of treatment appears to be *the perception of the non-using spouse*. If (s)he perceives the use of porn as problematic, it is.

Conjoint Marital Therapy

Coop Gordon, Baucom, Snyder and Dixon (2008) outline a three stage process for couple's treatment of infidelity. The authors stress the need to conceptualize the discovery of the affair (porn usage, for our purposes) as a traumatic event (p. 433). Acceptance of this characterization of the discovery allows therapists to fully grasp the cognitive, emotional, and behavioral disruption and damage it causes.

The structure of therapy presented by Coop Gordon, Baucom, Snyder and Dixon (2008) must involve both partners, as that allows for a thorough and careful exploration of individual contributions to the context of the porn usage. The primary client in this work is the relationship itself. Therapists should be cautioned that work of this nature is contraindicated if there is significant interpersonal violence occurring which the non-using partner is not willing to address. The authors suggest that individual sessions with each partner may prove helpful, provided clear expectations of confidentiality are identified (p. 433). Prior to beginning treatment of the couple, but after some initial assessment has been completed, it is important for the therapist to ask the couple for specific goals for treatment. Often the most salient goal is clarifying the intention of the partners for the future of the relationship: stay in relationship, terminate relationship, or wait and see. Some ambivalence or apprehension about the future of the relationship is to be expected, and it often serves as a useful starting point to discuss the process of therapy and reinforce that the goal of therapy is to support, maintain, and enhance the relationship *if it is healthy for both partners to do so*. Often when dealing with pornography, non-using partners feel completely betrayed in a way that they never anticipated. For example, women report that they would know how to feel about partner betrayal with another woman, but are unsure how they feel about multiple virtual women (Bridges, Bergner & Hesson-McInnis, p. 3).

The three stage process outlined by the authors includes dealing with the impact (of the porn use), finding meaning, and moving on (Coop Gordon, Baucom, Snyder and Dixon, p. 440). The integrative approach "strategically draws from cognitive-behavioral interventions, insight-oriented approaches and forgiveness and traumatic response literatures" ultimately resulting in a comprehensive yet flexible approach (p. 433). Dealing with the impact includes assessment of: the couple relationship; the outside affair relationship (here, the duration, frequency, and type of pornography consumed, in what settings); individual strengths and vulnerabilities; outside stressors and resources. Additionally, boundary setting, self-care and affect regulation, and coping with flashbacks are all tasks in this stage. Stage two, finding meaning, includes exploration of factors contributing to the porn usage, specifically relationship factors, external contributors (i.e., work, extended family), and individual aspects of each partner, and, relationship work. Relationship work is defined as directed problem solving and targeted homework assignments (p. 440). The final stage in this process, moving on, involves examination of forgiveness, including potential costs and benefits of forgiving and moving on, exploration of factors affecting decision to continue or terminate relationship, and further targeted relationship work, or preparation for termination of therapy.

The authors identify several factors related to couples' potential to recover from the discovery of heavy pornography usage. First, a high level of remorse on the part of the using partner is shown to be correlated with increased effectiveness of therapy (Coop Gordon, Baucom, Snyder & Dixon, p 431). High levels of remorse are often found amongst individuals who are more satisfied in general with their marriage. Additionally, couples with lower marital satisfaction, lower commitment to marriage in general, and shorter length of marriage was all correlated with less successful therapy. Perhaps the most indicative element of a couple's potential to heal from pornography usage is their ability to communicate openly and honestly about it. Couples who are able to process the traumatic event candidly are more likely to recover from the trauma (p. 431).

Zitzman and Butler (2005) explored the use of conjoint marital therapy with married couples recovering from husbands' addictive use of pornography. The authors distill the process into a concise statement: the goal is to "organize relationship to sponsor recovery while promoting essential relationship and individual healing for both spouses" (p. 311). Significant effects of conjoint marital therapy for this problem include: mutual softening of partners, increased marital trust, increased confidence in the future, and client perceived marital enhancement (p. 330). This research was conducted at Brigham Young University, and the authors suggest that the population sample studied, specifically devout Christians, may have had an effect on the data.

Ayres and Haddock (2009) explored treatment approaches dealing specifically with couples presenting online pornography consumption as an aspect of the current problem. The researchers presented 99 clinical members of the American Association of Marriage and Family Therapists with a vignette describing a presenting couple and measured adherence to specific treatment protocols. Researchers developed a coding scheme to evaluate therapist responses in two areas: assessment and hypotheses, and treatment planning. The authors hypothesized that several factors would affect therapeutic approach, including graduate training specifically for this kind of issue, feminist orientation, familiarity with literature on the topic, and personal attitudes toward pornography. The authors found that 75% of clinicians surveyed had encountered distress, either individual or interpersonal/relational, specifically related to consumption of pornography, in practice. However, a significant majority of those therapists report feeling 'completely unprepared' to deal with pornography as an interpersonal issue (p. 71). Additionally, two very significant self-of-the-therapist issues arose from the research, namely that the definition of what is pornographic must be provided by the client, and secondly, that a therapists personal viewpoint about pornography, more than any other factor explored in the research, determines level of adherence to high quality interventions (p. 74).

The themes of high quality interventions identified by the authors were not empirically tested, but rather compiled from an extensive review of research focused on sexual compulsions, addictions and its consequences. First, the authors suggest conducting a thorough assessment of pornography use and the potential for sexual addiction. Second, the therapist should place responsibility for change on the user and couples relationship, not on partner. When addiction is diagnosed, the focus of treatment must be on termination of use and then underlying couple dynamics. Lastly, therapists are reminded of the importance of validating the non-using partners' distress, and urged to engage the couple in a discussion about the 'culture' of pornography and how to respond to this culture (Ayers & Haddock, p.72). These themes do not represent a treatment plan per se, but rather guidelines which have been shown to correlate with successful outcomes dealing with the issue of pornography in relationships.

Atwood and Schwartz (2002) outlined a treatment process similar to the method discussed previously. The authors identified three types of cyber-sex: the cyber-flirt, cyber-sex, and the cyber-affair (p. 42). These concepts differ significantly from our focus, specifically that they require interaction with another person, albeit 'virtually'. Treatment involves evaluation, crisis intervention, dealing with underlying issues, building communication, and rebuilding marital trust. Two additional components not presented previously include constructing new stories and ritual for a fresh start (p. 52). The parallel nature of treatment approaches underscores the idea that it is not the extent of involvement in online sexual material which defines treatment, but rather the relational impact of such activity.

Self of the Therapist Issues

It is clear from the research that we, as clinicians, must not only be comfortable addressing and discussing pornography as an entity, but we also should fully explore our own biases regarding the material. Research by Goldberg, Peterson, Rosen and Sara (2008) indicate that the majority of marriage and family therapists are dealing with the issue of pornography interpersonally and/or individually, and that the numbers are increasing (p. 475). Ayres and Haddock (2009) suggested that marriage and family therapists' attitudes about pornography, above all other variables, influence treatment approach and adherence to recommended treatment protocols (p. 55). Other variables identified which did not influence treatment included graduate training specifically about pornography usage, familiarity with literature on topic, or a feminist orientation (p. 63).

Interestingly, the research by Ayres and Haddock (2009) suggests that a *more relaxed* attitude about pornography in general led to diminished adherence to recommended treatment protocols. Therapists who held a more positive general viewpoint regarding pornography were less likely to conduct further assessment of pornography use, less likely to consider that porn usage may be a problem, and more likely to place responsibility on female partner (p. 74). It appears that a blanket accepting attitude regarding usage of pornographic material is not always the most productive therapeutic stance. It is widely accepted that therapists' beliefs influence therapeutic approaches (Aponte, 1994). Davies (1996) underscored the key importance of therapists engaging in personal values clarification as a means of reducing projection of therapists own issues onto the client, and preventing omission of vital components of assessment or intervention. More than ever, it appears, therapists must evaluate our personal feelings and thoughts about pornography. No longer confined to the pages of a brown paper covered magazine, pornography lives in our homes and in our relationships. The ubiquity of the material must not be parlayed into blanket acceptance, lest we become de-sensitized to the impact, and blind to the interpersonal consequences.

Joan D. Atwood, Ph.D., LMFT, LCSW & Conchetta Gallo, Ph.D., LMFT

Suggestions for future research

Several areas in need of investigation have been identified throughout this paper. The impact of pornography usage by men has been researched, but the cumulative effects of a lifetime of exposure should be explored. How are men who have been raised in a culture of porn different from men who begin exposure in adulthood? Are their views about women and relationships significantly different? What relationship, if any, exists between sexual dysfunctions (erectile dysfunction, delayed ejaculation) and porn usage for men?

Not surprisingly, women have been virtually omitted from the research conversations about porn usage. How many women consume porn on a regular basis and how has it influenced their approach to interpersonal intimacy? Does porn influence women's feelings about appearance? Does porn affect a woman's concept of beauty, sexuality or monogamy? Does porn usage affect how women feel about, and approach, motherhood? How are adolescent girls affected by a culture of porn? Clearly, this is an area in dire need of empirical examination.

As identified in the study by Ayres and Haddock (2009), the therapist herself is a significant factor related to successful treatment outcomes, or more specifically, the therapist's attitude about pornography in general. This research in particular should be replicated and expanded upon. As clinicians, we should be dedicated to the exploration of our biases surrounding this issue. What influences our preconceptions about pornography? What factors relate to our feelings of competence to treat this issue? What should training for therapists to deal with pornography look like?

Conclusion

In 1964, Supreme Court Justice Potter Stewart, in an attempt to identify obscenity and what should be unprotected under the First Amendment, stated he would cease to attempt to define obscenity, but that he 'knew it when he saw it' (Silver, 2003). Nearly five decades later, we as a society still struggle with pornography and its impact on our culture and our lives. In some ways, the academic discussion about the topic parallels concepts of substance use, abuse and addiction. As marriage and family therapists, we are hard pressed to define when drinking becomes alcoholism, or when recreational drug use morphs into addiction. We must approach pornography in the same manner. The material itself is not the problem; problems with pornography arise from the meaning we attach to the material and its context within any one relationship.

References

Abell, J. W., Steenbergh, T. A., & Boivin, M. J. (2006). Cyberporn use in the context of religiosity. *Journal of Psychology and Theology, 34,* 165-171.

Albright, J. (2008). Sex in America online: an exploration of sex, marital status, and sexual identity in internet sex seeking and its impacts. *Journal of Sex Research, 45*(2), 175-186.

Aponte, H. (1994). How personal can training get? *Journal of Marital and Family Therapy, 20,* 1-16.

Atwood, J. D. & Schwartz, L. (2002). Cyber-sex—the new affair treatment considerations. *Journal of Couple & Relationship Therapy: Innovations in Clinical and Educational Interventions, 1*(3), 37-56.

Ayres, M. & Haddock, S. (2009). Therapists' approaches in working with heterosexual couples struggling with male partners' online sexual behavior. *Sexual Addiction & Compulsivity, 16,* 55-78.

Baltazar, A., Helm Jr., H., Mcbride, D., Hopkins, G., & Stevens Jr., J. (2010). Internet pornography use in the context of external and internal religiosity. *Journal of Psychology & Theology, 38*(1), 32-40.

Benjamin, O., & Tlusten, D. (2010). Intimacy and/or degradation: Heterosexual images of togetherness and women's embracement of pornography. *Sexualities, 13*(5), 599-623.

Bergner, R. & Bridges, A. (2002). The significance of heavy pornography involvement for romantic partners: research and clinical implications. *Journal of Sex & Marital Therapy, 28,* 193-206.

Bridges, A., Bergner, R. & Hesson-McInnis, M. (2003). Romantic partners' use of pornography: its significance for women. *Journal of Sex & Marital Therapy, 29,* 1-14.

Coop Gordon, K., Baucom, D., Snyder, D. & Dixon, L. (2008). Couple therapy and the treatment of affairs. In A. Gurman (Ed.), *Clinical Handbook of Couple Therapy* (pp.429-458). New York: Guilford Press.

Cooper, A. (2000). *Cybersex: The dark side of the force: A special issue of the journal of sexual addiction and compulsion.* New York: Brunner-Routledge.

Cooper, A., Delmonico, D. L., & Burg, R. (2000). Cybersex users, abusers, and compulsives: New findings and implications. *Sexual Addiction & Compulsivity*, 7, 5-29.

Cooper, A., Delmonico, D.L., Griffin-Shelley, E., & Mathy, R. M. (2004). Online sexual activity: an examination of potentially problematic behaviors. *Sexual Addiction & Compulsivity*, *11*, 129-143.

Cooper A., Galbreath N., & Becker, M. (2004). Sex on the internet: furthering our understanding of men with online sexual problems. *Psychology of Addictive Behaviors*, *18*(3), 223-30.

Cooper, A., Morahan-Martin, J., Mathy, J., & Maheu, M. (2002). Toward an increased understanding of user demographics in online sexual activities. *Journal of Sex and Marital Therapy*, *28*, 105-129.

CjNet. (2001). Net vices. CjNet. Retrieved from http://www.cnet.com/4520-6022_1-105202-1.html

Davies, D. (1996). Towards a model of gay affirmative therapy. In D. Davies & C. Neal (Eds.), *Pink therapy: a guide for counselors and therapists working with lesbian, gay and bisexual clients.* Buckingham: Open University.

Eaton, A. (2007). A Sensible Antiporn Feminism. *Ethics*, *117*(4), 674-715.

Goldberg, P., Peterson, B., Rosen, K. & Sara, M. L. (2008). Cybersex: the impact of a contemporary problem on the practices of marriage and family therapists. *Journal of Marital and Family Therapy*, *34* (4), 469-480.

Levert, N. P. (2007). A comparison of Christian and non-Christian males, authoritarianism, and their relationship to Internet pornography addiction/compulsion. *Sexual Addiction & Compulsivity, 14*, 145-166.

Manning, J. (2006). The Impact of Internet Pornography on Marriage and the Family: A Review of the Research. *Sexual Addiction & Compulsivity, 13*(2/3), 131-165.

McNair, B. (2002). *Striptease culture.* London: Routledge.

Oddone-Paolucci, E., Genius, M., & Violato, C. (2000). A meta-analysis of the published research on the effects of pornography. *The Changing Family and Child Development*, 48-59.

Philaretou, A. G., Mahfouz, A. Y., & Allen, K. R. (2005). Use of Internet pornography and men's well-being. *International Journal of Men's Health, 4*, 149-169.

Schneider, J. (2000). Effects of cybersex addiction on the family: results of a survey. *Sexual Addiction & Compulsivity, 7*(1/2), 31-58.

Shaw, S. M. (1999). Men's leisure and women's lives: the impact of pornography on women. *Leisure Studies, 18*, 197-212.

Silver, J. (2003) *Movie Day at the Supreme Court or "I know it when I see it": A History of the definition of obscenity.* Retrieved from http://library.findlaw.com

Simmons, C., Lehmann, P., & Collier-Tenison, S. (2008). Men's use of controlling behaviors: a comparison of reports by women in a domestic violence shelter and women in a domestic violence offender program. *Journal of Family Violence, 23*(6), 387-394.

Stack, S., Wasserman, I., & Kern, R. (2004). Adult social bonds and use of internet pornography. *Social Science Quarterly, 85*(1), 75-88.

Underwood, Heather & Findlay, Bruce. (2004) Internet relationships and their impact on primary relationships. *Behaviour Change, 21*(2), 127-140.

White, M., & Kimball, T. (2009). Attributes of Christian couples with a sexual addiction to internet pornography. *Journal of Psychology & Christianity, 28*(4), 350-359.

Whitty, M. (2002). Online infidelity: Is cybersex a real act of betrayal? Paper presented at 8th annual meeting of Society of Australian Social Psychologists, Adelaide, Australia.

Whitty, M. T. (2003). Pushing the wrong buttons: Men's and women's attitudes toward online and offline infidelity. *Cyberpsychology & Behavior, 6,* 569-579.

Zillman, D. & Bryant, J. (1984). Effects of massive exposure to pornography. In N.M. Malamuth & E. Donnerstein (Eds.), *Pornography and sexual aggression* (p. 115-138). Orlando, FL: Academic.

Zillman, D. & Bryant, J. (1988b). Effects of prolonged consumption of pornography on family values. *Journal of Family Issues, 9* (4), 518-544.

Zitzman, S. & Butler, M. (2005). Attachment, addiction, and recovery: conjoint marital therapy for recovery from a sexual addiction. *Sexual Addiction & Compulsivity, 12,* 311-337.

CHAPTER 8

Couples Dealing with Heavy Pornography Use

Jennifer Aull

This paper considers the case of a couple struggling with one partner's heavy internet pornography use. While this is a current and common problem there is a lack research into the meaning and challenges of this particular type of compulsion. The literature also fails to offer many therapeutic interventions specific to this issue. This paper tries to provide a look at what research is available and some suggestions with how this issue might be handled, primarily from a systemic couple's perspective.

Joan D. Atwood, Ph.D., LMFT, LCSW & Conchetta Gallo, Ph.D., LMFT

Introduction

Pornographic images have been available since well before the advent of the internet, but the internet has made pornography so much more accessible and available. For someone who struggles with controlling themselves in relation to pornography, the internet is a serious challenge. Heavy pornography use can become problematic, particularly for the romantic partners of those involved. What constitutes a problem? How much pornography use is too much?

Literature Review

When reviewing the literature around excessive pornography use two things become clear very quickly. The literature is lacking. There has not been enough research and what research has been done lacks therapeutic implications. There is also some difficulty in defining what some call cybersex addiction. Often the literature lumps all types of unwanted and problematic online sex related activities under the heading of cybersex or cybersex affairs. Some of the literature includes excessive pornography use or pornography addiction under this heading while other articles only include interactive internet based sexual activity under this heading.

This paper focuses only on excessive pornography use or pornography addiction that is online based. Often this activity escalates into interactive online sexual activity, but not always. According to Young (2006), "This process can fall into five successive and interdependent stages: discovery, experimentation, escalation, compulsion, and hopelessness. The stages are interdependent and highlight how users use the Internet as a progressive means of escape as part of an addiction cycle." (p.26) Most of the literature treats pornography addiction more as an addiction process, while cybersex affairs are treated more as traditional extramarital affairs. Excessive pornography use generally leads to escalation. "In the escalation stage, the behavior becomes more chronic and pronounced such that the addict becomes saturated with a continuous stream of sexual content that can take on riskier and riskier forms." (Young, 2006, p.31)

Part of the difficulty begins in trying to define a behavior based addiction. "The clinical perception of a sexual addiction is based on behaviors that obviously destructive to somebody—the person himself or herself, the spouse, the lover, family, employer or society." (Levine,2010,p.

262) Some define this type of addiction as a individual compulsivity or impulse control issue, while others place this as a relational issue that must be addressed within the context of a couple. "Because sexual compulsivity, like chemical dependency, is a family disease, the spouse of the sexual addict needs treatment for his/her excessive dependency on the addict. The can be viewed as enmeshed in an addictive family system in which the coaddict supports the addict's addiction." (Schneider, 1989, p. 289)

One study looked at the impact of heavy pornography usage on the partner. This study found that for most part the new information that their romantic partner was involved in heavy pornography use caused them to have a new view of the relationship, a new view of themselves and a new view of the partner. "Often, the discovery is connected to and seems to explain, other observations that the woman has been making. Most notable among these may be that her partner seems increasingly withdrawn and even secretive, and the observation that the quality of their sexual relationship has deteriorated." (Bergner, 2002, p.196)

Most of the partners in the study began questioning their sexual desirability. Most also viewed their pornography using partners in a new, more negative light. Some now categorized their partners as sexual perverts and or as inadequate fathers. "A second critical factor affecting both the woman's view of her partner and her willingness to stay in the relationship was the degree to which she perceived him as repentant for his behavior." (Bergner,2002, p. 200)

The relationship is also thrown into a new light, as well. "The vast majority of women in this study used words such as 'betrayal', 'cheating' and 'affair' to describe the significance that their partners involvement in pornography had for them. Although their partners were not in actual contact with other females, these women clearly viewed the pornographic activities as a form of infidelity." (Bergner, 2002, p.196) Later studies have concluded that this reassessment of self, partner and relationship is not as representative of partners struggling with their romantic partner's heavy pornography use as previous thought. "Nonetheless, of considerable interest is the fact that, within this broader mildly positive outlook, a substantial minority (approximately one third) of women did report that they ascribed highly negative meanings to, and experienced considerable distress over, their partner's use of pornography." (Bridges,2003, p.13) Though these two studies draw somewhat different conclusions, but both identify a group of women with partners whose heavy use of pornography causes significant difficulty in their relationships. This provides a basis for the need for more therapeutic interventions with couples seeking help around issues of heavy pornography use.

Among the few studies of couple's therapy used to address heavy pornography use, a number of conclusions have been drawn. A study from 2009 that looked at heterosexual couples where the female was struggling with the male's pornography use, some significant therapeutic guidelines came to light. "First, therapists are encouraged to conduct a thorough assessment of the pornography use and potential for sexual addiction." (Ayres, 2009, p.59) This study also recommended placing the onus for change both on the pornography user and on the relationship. The therapist should be careful not to pathologize the partner of the heavy pornography user. "Third, it is recommended that when an addiction or compulsion is diagnosed and the user's partner is reporting distress in the relationship, a focus of treatment needs to be on assisting the pornography user in terminating porn use, and subsequently attending to underlying couple dynamics that may need attention." (Ayres, 2009, p.59) Validating feelings should be included in this process as well as discussing and responding to the culture of pornography. This study seems to use a common understanding of the role of pornography in the relationship as a starting point. What if one partner believes that his pornography use is within appropriate limits while the other partner believes that this level of pornography use constitutes a compulsion or addiction? How can the therapist help a couple find common ground when their understanding of the role of pornography in their relationship is so different?

Another study from 2005, suggested that while recovery from problematic pornography usage is important, that the primary focus of marital therapy in these situations should be the couple and their distress. The therapy used in this study was found to . . . "demonstrate an increase in (a) marital trust and confidence in the future, (b) mutual softening, (c) the ability to discern key points of intervention sponsoring and supporting recovery, and (d) client-perceived marital enhancement." (Zitzman, 2005, p.311) This study concluded that marital therapy was an important part of any recovery from excessive pornography use. This therapy addressed the restoration of trust and open and honest communication. Several of the couples involved in the study reported that having someone else, in this case the therapist, as a witness to what was occurring was helpful. The monitoring of progress as well as the lessening of policing on the part of the spouse was also found to contribute to success.

There is a need for more literature on the topic of excessive pornography use and its effects on couples. More research on the effects on couples in this situation needs to be done, especially with couples who are not currently in distress. Once more of this research is in place, then various therapeutic methods need to be study as to their effectiveness with helping couples with pornography issues. This is an area for much future study and interest.

Case Presentation

Maggie called a Marriage and Family Therapist seeking help with what she described as her husband Bill's infidelity. Bill usually paid the credit card bill, but this month he had been away on a business trip for three weeks and so Maggie had opened the bill. When she did she discovered a number of charges that she did not recognize. She found that they were charges from various pornographic websites. Maggie then looked into the history on their shared home computer and found that it had been cleared. Maggie called Bill at his hotel in Cleveland at midnight in a rage, accusing Bill of all sorts of things including in-person infidelity. Bill denied it all and tried to get Maggie to believe she was confused. When he returned from his trip he admitted to Maggie that he was struggling with what he described as a porn addiction. Bill said that he had struggled with this in the past, but that the problem had started again recently, just after he received his diagnosis of a heart problem. Bill said that looking at porn helped to relieve his stress and that he was really struggling with the news of the heart problem.

Maggie was quite upset with this admission, but she told him she wanted to work on it. She wasn't sure she could ever trust him again, but she thought that he needed help. Bill agreed to go to therapy. Maggie and Bill have been married for three years and have one child age one. Maggie works part-time outside the home as a librarian and also cares for their daughter. Bill is an attorney who works long hours. Maggie described their marriage and lives as relatively happy until recently when they were both surprised when Bill received a diagnosis of a heart problem that might require surgery and was causing him to limit his usual active life style.

Joan D. Atwood, Ph.D., LMFT, LCSW & Conchetta Gallo, Ph.D., LMFT

DSM Diagnosis

Providing a DSM diagnosis, in this case, provides several challenges. First, this problem is truly a systemic couples issue and needs to be accessed from a systemic perspective. If this concern is put aside and the situation assessed from an individual perspective, this would most likely present as a sexual addiction or addiction to pornography. There is some discussion of including a listing like this in the DSM-V, but at this time no such listing exists. The future listing for pornography or sexual addiction will mostly likely resemble 312.31 Pathological Gambling. This diagnosis is also an impulse control addiction with a number of the same features. Imagining what this new listing might look like by adapting the Pathological Gambling diagnosis criteria to address pornography addiction, we would get:

A persistent and recurrent maladaptive gambling behavior as indicated by five (or more) of the following:

(1) is preoccupied with pornography.

(2) needs to view more violent and extreme forms of pornography to achieve the same effect.

(3) has repeated unsuccessful efforts to control, cut back, or stop viewing excessive amounts of pornography.

(4) is restless or irritable when attempting to cut down or stop viewing excessive amounts of pornography.

(5) views pornography as a way of escaping from problems or of relieving a dysphoric mood.

(6) after viewing excessive amounts of pornography one day, believes that the next day pornography use can be control

(7) lies to family members, therapist, or others to conceal the extent of involvement with pornography.

(8) has committed illegal acts such as forgery, fraud, theft, or embezzlement to finance pornography use.

(9) has jeopardized or lost a significant relationship, job, or educational or career opportunity because of pornography.

(10) relies on others to cover the results of excessive pornography viewing.

Of course, this diagnosis does not exist yet. In its place the diagnosis of 312.30 Impulse-Control Disorder Not Otherwise Specified could be used. This diagnosis would include the following subtypes: Lifelong type and generalized type meaning that this disorder has been an issue over the course of the person's life and that the issue does not present itself with just one partner or with one type of stimulation.

Systemic Diagnosis

A systemic diagnosis focuses less on the individual addiction issues and instead places the relationship at the center of the diagnosis. While keeping the couple and their relationship at the center, there are still multiple ways to diagnosis this couple's situation. Any diagnosis would need to address both the difficulty that Bill's porn usage has caused as well as the stress brought on by Bill's recent heart diagnosis.

In order to make a systemic diagnosis more information would need to be collected during the initial session. Both Bill and Maggie would need to have an opportunity to share what concerns what brought them to therapy in the first place. This allows each person to felt heard, but it also provides the therapist with valuable information about how each person sees the relationship. As each person shares their concerns the spouse is able to hear the others perspective, hopefully without becoming too defensive. Once Maggie and Bill have had their say, it is important to move quickly on to collecting more information for the assessment. How has their sex life been over the years? Do they have children? What works in their relationship both currently and in the past?

Treatment Goals

In this case, it would be easy to place the focus on the issue of heavy pornography use and the couple's sex life, but that would be a mistake. The first treatment goal is for each person of the couple of get the opportunity to share their point of view. Once they have both had an opportunity to be heard, then the goals becomes healing as a couple.

One of the first goals will be renewing trust. While the pornography usage will not be the only trust issue, it with be a central one. During this part of the therapy, a careful line will have to be monitored. Some information about Bill's "porn addiction" will need to be shared in order for Maggie to regain trust. At the same time, too much information about this perceived betrayal can cause undue damage. The therapist may want to have some individual sessions with the person struggling with pornography, but it must be clear to both people that no secrets will be shared. Maggie will need to feel as if Bill has shared enough that he is sincere about changing his ways, but too much information will just create an increase in Maggie's sense of betrayal and possible inferiority.

The rebuilding of trust will be a continued throughout therapy and beyond, but once a small amount of trust has been reestablished, the therapy should move to helping both Maggie and Bill to have a greater understanding of one another's experience. Bill will need to hear some of what it was like for Maggie to have a husband who was addicted to pornography. Maggie will need to hear what Bill's experience of receiving the heart diagnosis has been like. Has he felt supported? Is he scared? The therapist will need to help each person feel understood by restating their experience back to each of them. The therapist also needs to guide the couple in active listening of one another. The goal of understanding each other's experience is for healing to take place, but also for the couple to gain the skill of listening for the other's experience. Empathy for the other can be learned and practiced so that in the future there can be greater understanding.

The couple will eventually, hopefully, move toward a place of forgiveness. This may be helped by having a plan of action for going forward. In the case of the excessive pornography use, nothing will help with forgiveness as much as seeing an effort to change. If the couple is able to agree upon a plan for change that includes both changes on Bill's part in relation to pornography as well as a plan for Maggie to reduce her policing of the situation and they are able to see one another trying, there is a good chance that forgiveness will begin.

At this point another useful step would be to help both Bill and Maggie to reframe both the pornography problem as well as the heart diagnosis. Possible the pornography problem is best seen as a disease that Maggie can help Bill fight? Another possible reframe is to see pornography as a culture that Bill and Maggie do not want to participate in? While we don't want to demonize pornography, it may be helpful to see it as something that is an outside force that creates trouble for them as a couple. Bill still needs to take some personal responsibility, but by seeing the pornography problem as an external challenge the shame may be reduced. Some psycho education on the troubles with pornography use and the prevalence may be helpful as well.

As with almost all couple's therapy it is important to address communication skills and emotional intimacy. Some exercises around improving communication will be helpful. The sex life of the couple will also need to be addressed and some healing may need to take place in this area as well. Before reducing the number of therapy sessions the couple will want to have a relapse plan in place. What will they do if the pornography use increases again or if there is lying around the pornography use? How will the couple proceed with the news of the heart diagnosis? How can they support one another or find outside support if the heart condition worsens?

Systemic Interventions

A number of theoretical perspectives could be used to help the couple regain trust, learn more communication skills, increase intimacy, and feel heard and understood. In this case, Imago Couple's therapy may best address the overall health of their relationship. The therapy would have a positive perspective, helping the couple to have a conscious marriage.

The therapy would need to begin with a time for both individuals to voice their complaints and concerns. Once this was accomplished the therapist could help them to remember what originally drew them to each other. These descriptions will help the therapist to access the level of commitment and interest that are present in the couple. Before the initial session is over the therapist could give some general information about Imago therapy and ask the couple to create a relationship vision, to be shared with one another during the next session.

Maggie and Bill returned the next week with their respective relationship visions. As they went over them, they noticed that many of their desires for the relationship were the same. Both wanted to have fun together. Both wanted to have a happy child or possibly children in the future. Both mentioned wanting to be sexually faithful. Bob had mentioned wanting to feel loved and supported no matter his physical condition. While they had many shared items, the last two mentioned, sexual fidelity and Bill concerns about support if he is sick were subjects that needed to be discussed further.

The therapist asked the couple to hold onto these two items for the following session at which time they would try the Couple's dialogue. The therapist began the next session with a general description of how the Couple's dialogue works and then asked them to try it, first on something smaller, a small annoyance Maggie had felt with Bill that week.

Maggie: I would like to have a Couple's Dialogue. Is now okay?

Bill: I am available now.

Maggie: I felt ignored when you talked to you mother on the phone during dinner rather than asking if you could call back.

Bill: If I got it, you felt hurt when I talked to my mom on the phone during dinner, rather than calling back later. Did I get it?

Maggie: Yes.

Bill: Is there more about that?

Maggie: No, I think that's it.

Bill: OK, well I can understand why you might have been hurt or felt ignored when I talked to my mom in the middle of dinner.

Maggie: Yes

Bill: You feel ignored when I don't focus on our conversation during dinner. Is there anything else to that feeling?

Maggie: No, not really.

Bill: I would like to respond now. Is that okay?

Maggie: Sure

Bill: I don't usually make it a habit to talk to my mother if she calls during dinner, but she was having car trouble and I felt like this couldn't wait. I can see how it was frustrating for you.

Therapist: I can see by some of your facial expressions that this feels long handed and cumbersome, but it really does help, especially when it is something that is more difficult to talk about. It will give you a good opportunity to get in the habit of hearing one another and validating how the other one feels. I think it might be a good idea to try this with your desire for sexual fidelity. Let's start with you Bill.

The therapist then guided them through a contentious discussion about their desires for sexual fidelity in their relationships and what that looked like for both of them. This intervention helped them to discuss some of Bill's feelings about the pornography use. The same Couple's Dialogue format was used for Maggie and Bill to discuss Bill's heart problems and both of their feelings about that. Eventually the couple was able to go back and complete the Relationship Vision, which helped them to see that what they really wanted wasn't that different.

Several different Imago therapy interventions would prove to be helpful with this couple. At some point they would need to make a No-Exit decision. In this they would both commit to not exiting the relationship over the course of therapy. This may very well result in the closing of out of Bill's pornography use, but this would have to be a mutually agreed upon decision and it would only be for the time period they agreed upon. Many other Imago based interventions would be helpful for this couple as well.

At some point a more direct look at the couple's sex life may be in order. As trust is regained and forgiveness begins the sex life may naturally return to a more positive place. There is also an excellent chance that more sex therapy interventions may be needed to help the sex life either return to a better place or to move to a better place for the first time. Sensate focus exercises may be a good place for the couple to begin. While pornography can be very sexually stimulating, it is missing an in-person sensual component that only another person can provide. It may be helpful for the couple to begin slowly and for the pornography user to be reminded of some of the additional benefits of sex with a partner. If the couple are instructed to spend time enjoying one another with kissing and touching, but not to proceed to sex, they may feel more of a sexual connection.

Some of the Imago exercises that help to reignite the relationship may be suggested as well: the reromanticizing exercise, the surprise list or the fun list. In the reromanticizing exercise each person of the couple can come up with a list of kind things that the other person is already doing. By sharing these items with the other person they can be reminded of how they already care for one another. The couple can also make individual lists of how they have cared for one another in the past, but no longer do. For example, I used to feel loved a cared for when you pick me up from the airport after a business trip. Lastly the couple can come up with things that have never been done, but they would love the other partner to do for them. These items on these lists can be rated according to importance and then exchanged with the partner. Hopefully, this helps the couple to begin to think about way in which they should their caring to one another.

Alternative diagnosis

While continuing to look at the situation from a systemic point of view this case could be considered without any real emphasis on the heavy pornography usage. The case was presented with Bill describing his own problem as porn addiction. If instead there had been some disagreement in the level of the difficulty that pornography is causing in their lives, the diagnosis could have excluded the concern with pornography.

If, for example, Bill admitted to viewing pornography on a regular basis, but did not believe that this was a problem, some other issues could be placed at the center of the couple's diagnosis. Possibly Maggie's complaint about pornography is her attempt to explain a lack of sexual connection or dissatisfaction with the frequency. Possibly Maggie has jumped to the conclusion that the problem with their sex life is Bill's pornography use, but instead it is caused by a power struggle within the relationship. When Bill received the diagnosis of the heart condition, the power dynamic in the marriage changed. Maggie began treating Bill like he was less capable than he had been previously. Maggie had long felt held back by Bill's need to lead at almost all points in their marriage. The heart diagnosis had given Maggie the opportunity to take more control over their lives. Now Maggie and Bill are locked in the power struggle that has been brewing for years.

This power struggle is manifesting itself with disagreements over initiating sex, frequency of sex and how vigorous sex should be in light of

Bill's heart problem. The whole issue of sex has been become too problem laddened and contentious that it feels more like a battle at this point. Possibly if this power struggle can be resolved, the issue of the pornography use will be more manageable.

Conclusion

As the proliferation of internet pornography continues, the issue of heavy pornography use will continue to present itself in couple's therapy. Often times the partner of the heavy pornography user feels less attractive, less positive about the relationship in general and less motivated to engage in sex with their partner. Often the partner with the pornography issue feels overly controlled or monitored by their partner and they suffer from feelings of low self-worth related to their lack of self-control around pornography. All of these feelings can cause great strain to a relationship in general and to a couple's sex life. There is a great need for continued research in the area of pornography addiction and work with couples struggling with this problem.

References

Adams, K.M. & Robinson, D.W. (2001). Shame reduction, affect regulation, and sexual boundary development: Essential building blocks of sexual addiction treatment. *Sexual Addiction & Compulsivity*, 8, 23-44.

Ayres, M.M. & Haddock, S.A. (2009). Therapists' approaches in working with heterosexual couples struggling with male partners' online sexual behavior. *Sexual Addiction & Compulsivity*, 16, 55-78.

Bergner, R.M. & Bridges, A.J. (2002). The significance of heavy pornography involvement for romantic partners: Research and clinical implications. *Journal of Sex & Marital Therapy*, 28, 193-206.

Bergner, R.M., Bridges, A.J. & Hesson-Mcinnis. (2003). Romantic Partners' use of pornography: Its significance for women. *Journal of Sex & Marital Therapy*, 29, 1-14.

Butler, M.H. & Zitzman, S.T. (2005). Attachment, addiction, and recovery: Conjoint marital therapy for recovery from a sexual addiction. *Sexual Addiction & Compulsivity*, 12, 311-337.

Carvalheira, A. & Gomes, F.A. (2003). Cybersex in Portuguese chatrooms: A study of sexual behaviors related to online sex. *Journal of Sex & Marital Therapy*, 29, 345-360.

Cavaglion, G. (2008). Voices of coping in an Italian self-help virtual community of cyberporn dependents. CyberPsychology & Behavior, 11, 599-601.

Corley, M.D. & Schneider, J.P. (2002). Disclosing secrets: Guidelines for therapists working with sex addicts and co-addicts. *Sexual Addiction & Compulsivity*, 9, 43-67.

Edger, K. (2008). Book review: The porn trap. *Sexual Addiction & Compulsivity*, 15, 269-270.

Garrett, J., Landau, J. & Webb, R. (2008). Assisting a concerned person to motivate someone experiencing cybersex into treatment. *Journal of Marital and Family Therapy*, 34, 498-511.

Hendrix, H. (1988) *Getting the love you want: A guide for couples.*New York: Henry Holt & Co.

Kort, J. (2010). A review of "Getting off: pornography and end of masculinity". *Journal of Sex & Marital Therapy*, 36, 383-385.

Leiblum, S.R.(Ed.). (2007). *Principles and practice of sex therapy.* New York: The Guilford Press.

Levine, S.B. (2010). What is sexual addiction? *Journal of Sex & Marital Therapy*, 36, 261-275.

Maltz, L. & Maltz, W. (2008) *The porn trap: The essential guide to overcoming problems caused by pornography.* New York:Harper.

Marks, I. (1990). Behavioural (non-chemical) addictions. *British Journal of Addiction*, 85, 1389-1394.

Parker, T.S. & Wampler, K.S. (2003). How bad is it? Perceptions of the relationship impact of different types of internet sexual activities. *Contemporary Family Therapy*, 25,415-429.

Schneider, J. (2000). Effects of cybersex addiction on the family: Results of a survey. *Sexual Addiction & Compulsivity*, 7, 31-58.

Schneider, J. (1989). Rebuilding the marriage during recovery from compulsive sexual behavior. *Family Relations*, 38, 288-294.

Young, K. S. (2008). Internet sex addiction: Risks factors, stages of development, and treatment. *American Behavioral Scientist*, 52, 21-37.